A Manifesto for the Public University

A Manifesto for
the Public University

Edited by
JOHN HOLMWOOD

BLOOMSBURY ACADEMIC

First published in 2011 by
Bloomsbury Academic
an imprint of Bloomsbury Publishing Plc
50 Bedford Square, London WC1B 3DP, UK
and
175 Fifth Avenue, New York, NY 10010, USA

CIP records for this book are available from the
British Library and the Library of Congress

ISBN 978-1-84966-613-8 (paperback)
ISBN 978-1-84966-643-5 (ebook)

This book is produced using paper that is made from wood grown in managed, sustainable forests. It is natural, renewable and recyclable. The logging and manufacturing processes conform to the Environmental regulations of the country of origin.

Printed and bound in Great Britain by the MPG Books Group, Bodmin, Cornwall

Cover design: Burge Agency

www.bloomsburyacademic.com

Acknowledgements

This book was conceived some time ago after early indications that government plans for higher education were promising to be much more drastic than had been anticipated. Fearing the worst, some of us – university academics and graduate students – got together to form the Campaign for the Public University (*http://publicuniversity.org.uk*) to argue for the wider value of public higher education. I should like to thank those friends and colleagues – Gurminder K. Bhambra, Mark Carrigan, Michael Farrelly and Lucy Mayblin – for their commitment, activism and comradeship. Others have since joined the campaign and other campaigns have joined together. I should also like to thank Andrew McGettigan, Jan Balon, Bernard Sufrin, Kate Tunstall, Alex Smith, and, of course, my fellow contributors to this book. Finally, thanks, too, to Emily Salz and her colleagues at Bloomsbury Press for their patience, professionalism and persistence.

The book is dedicated to those students who, wanting a better future for themselves, also want it for others, and to the university staff that share the same aspiration.

Contents

Contributors

Michael Burawoy is Professor of Sociology at the University of California, Berkeley. He is an ethnographer of industrial workplaces and a leading advocate of public sociology. A former President of the American Sociological Association, he is currently President of the International Sociological Association.

John Holmwood is Professor of Sociology at the University of Nottingham and fellow of the Academy of Social Sciences. He is conducting research into the moral economy of inequality. He is Chair of the UK Council of Heads and Professors of Sociology and one of the founding members of the Campaign for the Public University.

Desmond King is Andrew W. Mellon Professor of Government at the University of Oxford and fellow of Nuffield College. He specializes in the study of the American state and in race and politics. He is a fellow of the British Academy.

Stephen McKay is Professor of Social Research at the University of Birmingham. He has interests in the study of wealth, inequality and social welfare.

Nicola Miller is Professor of Latin American History and Head of the History Department at University College, London. She researches intellectual history, cultural history and international history. She is a founder member of the Humanities Matter campaign.

Philip Moriarty is Professor of Physics at the University of Nottingham. His research interests are in nanoscience.

Diane Reay is Professor of Education at the University of Cambridge. Her research addresses issues of education and social justice, with particular reference to class, gender and ethnicities. She is a fellow of the Academy of the Social Sciences.

Karen Rowlingson is Professor of Social Policy and Director of the Centre on Household Assets and Savings Management at the University of Birmingham. Her research interests are in the financial security of individuals, families and households.

John Sabapathy is Lecturer in Medieval History at University College, London. His research interests are in administration, accountability and how institutions think. He is a founder member of the Humanities Matter campaign.

Sir Steve Smith is Professor of International Studies and Vice-Chancellor of Exeter University. Until July 2011 he was President of Universities UK, the representative organization for universities in the UK. He is a former president of the International Studies Association and is a fellow of the Academy of Social Sciences.

Introduction

John Holmwood

The present volume has a very specific moment of gestation, namely the perception in the United Kingdom of a crisis in the idea of the public university associated with the publication of the Browne Report in October 2010 (Browne Report 2010).[1] In effect, the Report recommended a higher education system directed by market forces and the replacement of direct funding of undergraduate courses by student fees. Students would be supported by a system of publicly funded loans, but their fees would replace the direct funding of undergraduate courses through the 'block grant' (except for high priority, or high cost, courses in science, engineering and medicine, where some direct funding would remain).

The recommendations were enthusiastically accepted by the new Conservative-Liberal Democrat coalition government, which had taken office in May 2010. It had formed an agreement to reduce dramatically the fiscal deficit caused by bailing out the financial sector following the financial crisis. It sought cuts to government spending across all departments (except health) in the region of 20–30 per cent. The removal of the 'block grant' and the shift in the cost of undergraduate education from the tax system to individual students via loans promised a reduction in spending on higher education of 80 per cent. Notwithstanding that the Liberal Democrats had opposed tuition fees as part of their election campaign, and that the Conservatives had made no mention of it in their campaign literature, the coalition pressed ahead with the proposals, albeit capping the upper level of fees at £9,000, and seeking mechanisms that would assure that such fees would not be typical and that a lower fee of £6,000 would stick in most cases.[2]

The proposals sent shock waves across higher education circles in the UK, including a very visible response from students in the form of demonstrations and campus occupations. University Vice-Chancellors, however, were muted in response. As Sir Steve Smith, President of the body representing universities, Universities UK, suggests in the afterword of this book, they were faced with the threat of very serious cuts to funding – around 20 to 30 per cent – and the opportunity to replace that cut by student fees seemed like a lifeline that would enable universities to get through a potentially very serious financial crisis without too much damage.

For many students and prospective students, the primary issue was the breach of an electoral promise and the absence of a proper debate. There was also the related issue that the government justified the cutting of the fiscal deficit as a duty, which the present generation owed future generations, not to leave to them a legacy of debt. Yet, it seemed that the act of privatizing undergraduate education involved just that, bequeathing high levels of indebtedness to future generations of students in a decision made by politicians who were nearly all beneficiaries of publicly funded higher education.

Moreover, it quite quickly became apparent that the costs of the new system of student loans would be similar to the savings made by cutting the block grant. The only difference was that, by an 'accounting device', the cost would appear to be 'off the books'. Indeed, in making this assessment, the independent Higher Education Policy Institute concluded that, 'the idea of the withdrawal of the state from the direct funding of universities is deeply ideological' (Thompson and Bekhradnia 2010: paragraph 52), and was specifically designed to introduce a market in higher education.

This book is written in direct response to the threat to the public benefits of higher education that will potentially follow from the introduction of the market.[3] One of the primary public goods afforded by universities is that of providing means of public debate. For that reason, an afterword by Sir Steve Smith is included. He suggests that the risks are not as severe as those claimed by the other authors in this volume and, more importantly, not as severe as the risks that would have followed from swingeing cuts to public funding with no alternative source of funding being made available. In the rest of this introduction, I shall set out some elements of the counter-argument, while recognizing that Sir Steve Smith's position has some merit and, potentially, has some support across the sector from academics at institutions likely to be beneficiaries. Nonetheless, the stakes are high.

At the outset, let me concede that although the idea of a public university is strongly associated with that of a publicly funded university, it would be difficult to claim that the association is a necessary one. The authors in this book define the public university in terms of its public benefits and, more specifically, how it functions for the public or publics, not directly by how it is funded, though all of us believe public funding to be justified. Nor is it the case that the only functions of a university are public functions. In Chapter 2, I will set out the development of the idea of the 'multiversity' (Kerr 2001 [1963]) and the place of the public functions of the university within it. I will also set out how the standard view of the 'public' makes the government its representative and the protector of its interests as taxpayer. In contrast, I shall use the pragmatist philosopher, John Dewey, to argue that the public is properly regarded as *representing itself*, with the university facilitating that representation through the encouragement of debate and common resources of knowledge.

Where the functions of the university are understood as multiple, this poses the issue of how their relations should be conceived, especially in the context of private interests in the commodification of knowledge and globalization of the economy and higher education. In Chapter 2, Michael Burawoy sets out different dimensions of the university and its audiences and how the marketization of higher education threatens the wider public good that the university can serve. The multiversity risks becoming a monoversity serving only private purposes, with its public functions atrophying.

While there is considerable overlap between the two ideas – public universities and public funding – universities necessarily also receive income from private sources and serve private benefits. Moreover, given the history of many universities as institutions founded by private endowments, it is difficult to suggest that their public benefits can only be secured by public funding. Historically, however, private universities have usually been charitable institutions organized on a 'not-for-profit' basis.

For the most part, there has been a broad political consensus on the value of public higher education. This has been evident for the past fifty or sixty years across countries that are otherwise very different in their public policy regimes. Indeed, most have recognized first secondary education, and then higher education, as social rights necessary to the achievement of other liberal rights, such as employment based on meritocratic achievement, and political participation.

What is distinctive at the present time, however, is the breakdown of this political consensus and the development of the idea that education is not something external to the market, upon which the latter's fair and proper functioning might depend, but something that may itself be subject to the market. Thus, the last decades have witnessed the emergence of 'for-profit' providers of higher education, in the form of transnational corporations (such as Apollo Group, Kaplan and Pearson International). These latter providers are not directed toward the public good, but shareholder value and executive packages, derived from offering a cheaper product that has 'stripped out' the public functions of higher education (except in so far as it is compatible with maximizing private returns). Indeed, it is precisely in order to facilitate competition by for-profit providers that the 'block grant' has been removed (McGettigan 2010).

In so far as other universities are required to compete on the same terms as for-profit providers, or find an 'added value' that can be sold to students as the source of a future private benefit, then the wider public benefits of higher education are at serious risk. The issue is not so much retaining (or increasing) current levels of funding for higher education – it is true that this can be done by student fees *or* by public funding – but the nature of the purposes of higher education and the consequences of allowing those purposes to be defined by the market.

The reforms to higher education that are currently taking place in England are not only about teaching, but also about research with the government pressing funding bodies – the Higher Education Funding Councils, and also the Research Councils – to emphasize concentration and selectivity in their distribution of funds, as well as to ensure increased impact of research for private users and other beneficiaries.

As Philip Moriarty (Chapter 4) indicates, the public funding of science is increasingly directed away from 'blue skies' research toward research that can show a direct benefit to a private beneficiary. According to Moriarty, this challenges the 'norms' intrinsic to the organization of science and to the maintenance of public trust. At the same time, most of the evidence about guiding science toward short-term economic gains suggests that it is a policy that will not deliver the outcomes that are sought. Paradoxically, the increased emphasis on the marketization of public research and development derives, in part, from market failure in private research and development.

It is difficult to resist the conclusion that for all the emphasis on 'evidence-based policy', governments are more interested in 'policy-based evidence'. This is traced by Desmond King in Chapter 5, where he sets the history of the Economic and Social Research Council (ESRC) and government pressures upon it. Whereas the provision of policy-relevant knowledge is widely recognized as one of the public functions of the university and one of the reasons for the public funding of research in the social sciences, what has been most difficult is the accommodation of this function to the changing political context of universities.

As King argues, while there was wide political acceptance that social scientific knowledge had an important function in public policy, only tentative steps were made to the institutionalizing of the idea that this knowledge might also serve critical purposes and be the means by which publics might hold governments to account. That governments seek to steer the development of social scientific research toward preferred ends is one seeming constant in the history of the ESRC. However, the shift to neo-liberal modes of governance of research seems to have extinguished any idea of social scientific knowledge facilitating public debate and criticism. In so far as universities adapt to the external context of research funding, this restriction becomes general across the sector.

The present book is a manifesto for the public university. However, a manifesto usually has an orientation to the future, setting out the changes that it wishes to bring into being. This manifesto also invokes the past, calling for changes to the current direction of higher education, in the name of well-established values that are being hollowed out by the market, notwithstanding government claims to promote a 'Big Society'. In doing so, we propose that the crisis of the public university is also a crisis of public life.

In part, this crisis in public life is indicated by the fact that the proposals for radical change in the organization of higher education in England had not been discussed prior to the election. The Browne Report itself was presented as the very substance of the debate, as the proposals on fees were 'whipped' through Parliament. Yet, as Baroness Tessa Blackstone, Vice-Chancellor of the University of Greenwich, commented in the short debate in the House of Lords:

> No-one could have predicted that such a review would double the fees then proposed and assume that the public funding of 80 per cent of undergraduate tuition would be abandoned. Nor would anyone have predicted that this review would be based on a commitment to the free market that is so extreme that it abandons, to quote Sir Peter Scott, a much respected vice-chancellor and former member of the HEFCE board, 'the very idea of a public system of higher education, built with such care and effort since Robbins'. (2010)

Reference to the Report of the Robbins Committee on Higher Education (1963) is apposite. The reforms challenge the principles established by that Committee, which have guided the development of UK higher education since that date. In effect, it recommended the expansion of higher education and its integration with the secondary school system. The Education Act of 1944 had extended the right of publicly funded secondary education to all and the Robbins Committee extended that right to higher education. This was enshrined in the axiom that, 'courses of higher education should be available for all those who are qualified by ability and attainment to pursue them and who wish to do so' (Robbins Report 1963: para. 31).

The Committee also recognized that the expansion of higher education served important economic ends (the Committee did not use the term 'knowledge economy', but it did recognize the increasing importance of the knowledge base to economic growth), as did the later Dearing Report of 1997, with its theme of the 'knowledge society'. In making these arguments, the Robbins Report was of the view that higher education had grown in an ad hoc way and in a variety of institutions (universities, colleges of education, colleges of advanced technology and colleges of further education), and was pursued by a variety of routes (full-time, part-time and sandwich courses). The Committee proposed to approach higher education as a *system* and recommended that there should be a diversity of institutions, with different characteristics, but that they should all be properly supported and allowed to flourish.

In part, the Robbins Committee was confronting the status hierarchy evident in a secondary school system divided in terms of public and private schools. These status differences were also to be found among universities, especially the ancient universities of Oxford and Cambridge, with their longstanding connections to the system of private secondary education. However, the expansion of higher education would mitigate these status differences by widening access and integrating public secondary education with a system of public higher education. While status differences among higher education institutions were likely to continue, for the Robbins Committee the purpose of the new system was to mitigate those differences. Yet, as Diane Reay argues (Chapter 7), these status differences have remained and the new system of funding is likely to reinforce them, with the intention to generate 'selective' institutions able to charge higher fees than less 'selective' institutions. Indeed, with the recommendation of a stratified system of selective universities each differently resourced, the idea of education shifts from being a 'public good' to a 'positional good', one enjoyed to the extent that it confers an exclusive advantage. In this way, selection is also social, and the consequence is to reinforce the social exclusivity of institutions and the social distance between different groups.

The immediate context of the Robbins Report was a perception that the UK lagged behind other countries – especially the United States and Western Europe – in terms of the proportion of the age cohort attending university. This was argued to be potentially damaging to UK economic performance in the context of increasing demand for a highly educated workforce. However, this was by no means the only justification put forward by Robbins. Education was seen as a public good in its own terms, valuable both for the student and the wider society. University education, according to Robbins, served to cultivate the mind, and was concerned with the development and transmission of knowledge and culture, as well as serving democratic citizenship by improving debate and the capacities of citizens (Robbins Report 1963: paras 25–8).

The Robbins Committee also argued that education should take place in an environment in which research (or scholarship) and teaching occur alongside each other. This would inculcate in students standards of criticism and rigour by example, but it was also right, Robbins argued, that universities should meet the aspirations of those who work in them to apply themselves to scholarship, research and the development of knowledge. It is precisely these broad concerns that are absent in the Browne Report and in government plans for the opening-up of the sector to for-profit providers, which are to be granted the title of university without having the functions or characteristics of a university in terms of research or teaching staff who have themselves participated in the development of the knowledge they seek to transmit. Nor, it must be said, have university vice-chancellors distinguished themselves by arguing vigorously for the very functions of the university and its modes of instruction that the Robbins Report defined as essential to education at degree level.

However, the simple expansion of the system, together with the increased emphasis on audit measures that have gone along with it, does indicate problems in the development of higher education, as Miller and Sabapathy discuss (Chapter 3). Students are rightly concerned with employment and have the expectation that going to university will help them secure the jobs to which they aspire. Nonetheless, university also helps students discover and expand their idea of themselves and how they might realize themselves within particular employments or make a difference. However, a concern with the reproduction of academic subjects – something of direct interest to academics and reinforced by the Research Assessment Exercise – does not serve an expanded idea of education either. In other words, while the marketization of undergraduate courses and 'student choice' are a poor means for securing this enlarged idea of education, it is also incumbent upon academic staff to develop a curriculum suited to the needs of students. In other words, it is right that students be at the heart of higher education, but in a role other than as consumers.

The expansion of student numbers took place gradually. A modest increase after the construction of new universities and the incorporation of the old colleges of advanced technology, following Robbins, accelerated from about 15 per cent in the 1980s to the present figure of around 36 per cent of eighteen- to nineteen-year-olds (the figure is higher if account is taken of students who enter when they are older).[4] This was accomplished, in part, by the incorporation of the polytechnics into the university system in 1992 (something intended by the Robbins Committee, but not initially accomplished due to opposition), but also by a general expansion of student numbers and increased exhortations to young people about the benefits of higher education (albeit usually couched in utilitarian terms).

It is not difficult to see that while the principle of publicly funded university education in the UK emerged in the 1960s as a prelude to the creation of a system of mass higher education, it seems to have been called into question by the further expansion of university education in the 1980s. This is a somewhat paradoxical development. The principle of publicly funded universal secondary education is not in doubt, despite its expansion. What seemed to give the members of the Browne Review some pause in seeing higher education in the same light is the qualification that lies in the Robbins' axiom, namely that it is a right that is to be limited by ability and attainment. It is this limitation that makes education beyond any compulsory school leaving age less than universal.[5] At the same time, it potentially reintroduces a possible new 'status' – perhaps, attainment is not equivalent and not all levels of attainment should be supported equally? In other words, the very mitigation of status differences among institutions of higher education promoted by the Robbins Committee has come to be challenged by the idea that higher education is properly 'selective', where more 'selective' institutions are deserving of greater support through the charging of higher fees (albeit the ultimate intention of higher fees is not that they should support better teaching, but other aspects of the 'student experience' and research).[6]

For Lord Browne and his colleagues, this further implied that there were benefits to higher education that accrued to individuals and that these were potentially different depending upon the institution attended and the subject studied. For Browne this also meant that any public funding of a degree programme was tantamount to a subsidy of a private benefit and potentially unjust. Yet this, too, was an argument addressed by the Robbins Committee, which allowed that it might warrant the student paying a contribution in the form of fees supported by loans. However, the Robbins Committee recommended against it on a number of grounds. First, it was argued that that the calculation of future benefit is too uncertain, given likely changes in the labour market. Second, it maintained that there were significant public goods secured by university education and that, for these reasons, public funding is appropriate. Indeed, not to recognize this would be a different kind of injustice, where private individuals would be asked to secure a public benefit (Robbins Report 1963: para. 644).

If the Dearing Report (1997) answered the question a little differently, recommending 'top up fees', it did so with a similar general orientation to the problem as that of the Robbins Committee. The public benefits of higher education extended beyond those of private individuals. Public higher education is necessary to 'sustain a culture which demands disciplined thinking, encourages curiosity, challenges existing ideas and generates new ones; [and to] be part of the conscience of a democratic society, founded on respect for the rights of the individual and the responsibilities of the individual to society as a whole' (Dearing Report 1997: para. 5). For this reason, fees paid by students should only be a supplement to publicly funded higher education.[7]

One of the troubling features of the Browne Report is its unbalanced nature. While it raises the 'injustice' of a public subsidy for a private benefit, it does not address the issue of the private subsidy of public benefits. Indeed, the 'philistine' nature of the Report identified by Collini (2010), which he associates with the reduction of all value to economic utility, can be understood as a tactical and cynical device.[8] The Report was expressly seeking to justify a market in higher education and the conversion of all public funding of arts, humanities and social science subjects into funding by student fees supported by a system of loans. To have identified the public benefits of higher education would be to imply the very case for public funding, just as the Report was seeking to present the opposite conclusion.

But why might the public funding of higher education be thought unsustainable in a context where the economic significance of education is increasingly recognized (Sainsbury Report 2007)? The expansion of higher education after Robbins was linked to another specific expectation. This was the assumption of a secular decline in the range of inequalities associated with a general increase in pay at the bottom and a relative reduction in returns at the top (brought about, in part, by the expansion of higher education). Notwithstanding Lord Robbins' own reputation as a liberal economist committed to the market mechanism where appropriate, this understanding of a progressive decline in inequality was central to his own perception of the wider environment in which higher education was developing. Since the 1980s, however, the secular decline in inequality has been sharply reversed, associated with neo-liberal policies of deregulation applied throughout the economy, such that inequalities are now more sharply polarized than at any time since the early 1900s. As Stephen McKay and Karen Rowlingson argue (Chapter 6), this structure of inequality is the context in which universities now function and any question of their 'social mission' has to take into account the fact that universities are themselves part of the reproduction of inequality.

With the increase in inequalities, however, has also come a reduction in taxation on high earners and a concern to target benefits on those who are most in need. In the context of education, this includes the idea that the public subsidy of higher education is not only a subsidy of those who will go on to benefit, but also of those whose families have paid for their children's secondary education (frequently at fees well in excess of those currently proposed for universities, even at the premium level of £9,000). The fact that some can afford to pay for their children's education – and wish to do so to secure an advantage for them – is converted into a requirement that all should pay. As McKay and Rowlingson argue, higher education as a social right is thereby diminished and represented as a 'choice', where current and future indebtedness will be a major constraint on participation for those from less well-off backgrounds.

Moreover, the contribution that universities might make to economic growth is now associated with an economy that is allowed to be an engine of inequality. It is this that motivates the introduction of the 'figure' of the manual worker who does not benefit from higher education, but is being asked to pay for it through taxation. Whereas the wider benefit was previously understood in terms of the general impact of education in reducing inequalities, and improving jobs, now it seems that the issue is one of social mobility within a system of widening inequalities. The issue has become how to secure greater participation in higher education of the 'manual worker's' children – through bursaries and support for children from poor backgrounds, for example – rather than the problem of poverty as such. However, the problem of poverty and inequality is precisely to make it difficult for those aspirations to be fulfilled, a situation that will be exacerbated by the new system of fees.

This is an attenuation of the social mission of the university and its contribution to citizenship, but it also has paradoxical consequences. Social mobility is more difficult precisely where inequality is greatest (Wilkinson and Pickett 2009). Where wide inequalities are tolerated, the emphasis is usually upon targeted (rather than universal) solutions to deal with specific problems, but these have unintended consequences that reinforce the problem of access. Education shifts from being a right of citizenship to a private investment in personal human capital and the transition from Robbins to Browne is complete. Whereas the success of the Robbins reforms was to 'universalize' the aspiration to higher education,[9] the current government's response is now to privatize higher education and thereby to reduce the opportunities to fulfil those aspirations.

The public university matters to everyone, we contend, because it is a condition of citizenship and full participation in economic, cultural and political life. Whatever diminishes it, diminishes our life in common.

1

The Idea of a Public University

John Holmwood

In this chapter, I want to address the idea of the public university – specifically, the functions that might be attributed to it – and to do so in the context of changes in the wider environment in which universities operate. I shall also examine the idea of the *public* (or publics), from which the modern university might derive its meaning as a *public* university. In doing so, I will draw on the work of the American pragmatist philosopher, John Dewey.

I shall also connect these functions to the theme of the 'Big Society', something promoted by the Prime Minister, David Cameron, as the alternative to 'Big Government' and the key idea behind reforms across a number of different sectors. I shall suggest that the problems associated with this idea derive from a failure to articulate the meaning of the public (or publics).

The problems I address are not new. Writing in 1963, Clark Kerr (2001 [1963]) set out the history of the modern research university – or 'multiversity' – as an institution sustained by contract research and continuous government grants. With increased public funding came an increased political interest in using that funding to direct the university towards meeting public policy objectives. For the most part, these came to be reduced to the twin objectives of securing economic growth and an educated workforce. However, for Kerr, the university also served a social mission. If this remained obscured by its other functions, the explanation was, in part, because the rise of mass higher education was also associated with a general societal process of democratic inclusion and a narrowing of economic inequalities.[1]

What is radically different about our own times, amid the continuities, is that for the first time the university is being addressed as an instrument

THE IDEA OF A PUBLIC UNIVERSITY 13

to extend social inequality. The promotion of the market mechanism in higher education is set to reproduce and solidify inequalities, rather than to dissolve them. We can no longer, then, avoid the issue of the university's social mission and, in particular, its role in social justice. Following Dewey, I shall argue that the problems of the public are problems of social justice. The failure of present policies and the debate that surrounds them is the common reduction of the university to instrumental functions.

The functions of a university

I do not intend to provide a detailed history of the university. An institution that can trace its origins to the thirteenth and fourteenth century, it has come to be a central part of the modern social order, and, in the course of that journey, it has drawn its character and functions from the wider environment in which it finds itself. A number of key functions have been attributed to the university from that, endorsed by Immanuel Kant and Alexander von Humboldt, of the university as a repository of reason and culture (as expressed by the humanities and the faculty of philosophy), to Cardinal John Henry Newman's idea of the university as a community engaged in the education of character and intellect (as expressed in the collegiate organization of Oxford and Cambridge). Whereas Humboldt argued for the importance of research alongside teaching, Newman saw no role for research within the university, believing it to be organized around utilitarian ends and to be something that could be pursued just as effectively outside the university, where it would not conflict with the latter's proper purposes.

These ideas of the university have a powerful hold, but were already in decline when Max Weber wrote his essay on 'science as a vocation' (1948 [1919]). According to him, scholarship and research were becoming more specialized and a university appointment was increasingly seen, not in terms of a 'vocation', but in terms of employment and a career embedded within a bureaucratic organization.[2] Weber was reflecting on the rise of the university in the United States and, in part, on the impact of the latter's democratic ethos, which encouraged a practical attitude to education and its value in everyday, commercial life. In contrast, the ideal of the pursuit of knowledge as a 'vocation' betrayed its origin as part of an upper-class status order to which others might aspire to be recruited (though not women or Jews – to the latter, Weber said, 'abandon all hope' of academic advancement [1948 (1919): 134] – and, of course, in the USA, unnoticed by Weber, not black Americans, who were to be 'segregated scholars' [Wilson 2006] until the 1960s).

For much of the twentieth century, the development of universities in the United States seemed to progress in a manner different to that of other countries. To be sure, the rise of the 'civic' universities in England and Wales from the late nineteenth century onwards, together with the rather different Scottish universities, had begun to loosen the hold of the collegiate idea of the university and its orientation toward the 'liberal professions'. As Sanderson argues, the new 'civic' universities were designed to meet the demands of local business elites (1972).[3] However, the hold of the collegiate idea was also evident in the Robbins Report (1963). It gave rise to the creation of seven 'new universities', which incorporated the collegiate idea into their organization and architecture. The idea that a university education was not simply about the transmission of skills, but also about a broader development of the individual which required interaction among teachers, who also pursued research, and among students, who were 'in residence' and part of a community of individuals pursuing courses of study together, was a central idea (which also became the norm for older civic universities, too).

The traditional idea of the university, as Weber acknowledged, served an elite status order. In England this involved an alignment of the private secondary schools, such as Eton, Harrow, Westminster and Winchester, with Oxbridge colleges, something also reflected in their common architecture of quadrangle, dining hall and chapel. A significant part of the history of the university in the twentieth century, then, is its accommodation to the transformation of that status order and the democratization of the wider society that it served. This is precisely the significance of the Robbins Report and its recommendation of a system of public higher education and its expansion.

Although the particularities of university and secondary school systems differ across countries and, indeed, in the case of the UK within them, too, there are similarities in how they have developed. Paradoxically, given its determinedly anti-elitist ethos, the United States is one of the few countries to have private universities – the 'ivy league' – alongside state-funded institutions (going back to the 'land grant' institutions introduced by President Lincoln). Otherwise, the dominant model is of publicly funded institutions. Some universities, like the publicly funded institutions of the United States, United Kingdom, Australia and New Zealand, also charge tuition fees to students (in contrast to the public funding of universal secondary education). With the charging of fees comes the attenuation of the residential idea of the university, as students combine study with part-time work and seek to reduce their costs by living at home and attending the 'local' university. It is in this context that the relatively equal status of different institutions becomes important, or else status differences also express the ability to pay. This is a very clear tension in the US system of higher education and one that the government is now seeking to introduce into Britain.[4]

At the same time that Lord Robbins delivered his report to the British Parliament, Clark Kerr, President of the University of California, delivered his Godkin lectures on the uses of the university (Kerr 2001 [1963]). He spoke of the transformation of the university into a 'multiversity'. He used this term to indicate the different functions, or uses, of the modern university and how it had been transformed from a single community into a multiplicity of communities, each reflecting its different functions. Kerr was also clear that while modern universities (and their academic constituencies) were jealous of their autonomy, they were also highly adaptive institutions. Most of the changes had taken place as a consequence of changes in the wider social environment, to which the university had adjusted, but in each case the adjustment had also been brought about by the active engagement of at least one of its constituent communities. This frequently gave rise to conflict within the multiversity, just in so far as a conflict of interest among its different constituencies was associated with shifts in the valuation of its different activities (for example, with regard to rewards of promotion, status and the like).

The multiversity, for Kerr, then, is necessarily pluralist, but also necessarily in tension. What is at issue, now, is the extent to which that plurality and tension is being resolved by the reduction of the university to the determination by the market and utility, where the university becomes not a multiversity but a monoversity; that is, neither a community in Newman's sense nor a plurality of communities in Kerr's, but a corporation delivering higher education.

Essentially, Kerr describes two broad trends. The first was a shift from the university concerned with teaching (associated with the liberal professions of law and religious ministry, and subsequently medicine) to one concerned with research (with its emphasis on postgraduate rather than undergraduate education). The second is the shift from higher education as the province of an elite (initially, of men) to it being made available for all as part of a mass education system that integrated secondary school education with higher education. Each development is associated with what Kerr called the 'knowledge industries'. These incorporated research and development as aspects of the corporate capitalist economy and, at the same time, increased the demand for an educated workforce (in effect, creating new professions and quasi-professions, based on university learning). However, the expansion of the mass education system was also associated with 'democratization', as education became seen as a right to be guaranteed by the state and equal opportunities became embodied within that right (although, of course, in the United States racially segregated higher education remained a reality, unremarked by Kerr when he first delivered his lectures).

Thus, a number of refractions separate Cardinal Newman's disparagement of research and its utility, in his expression of the essential idea of the university, from Clark Kerr's idea of the multiversity and its multiple utilities. Kerr's multiversity is a research university and it is located in a mass education system. With the rise of the knowledge economy it has also become increasingly an object of public policy. Where the university had previously been maintained by private and public endowments, the multiversity would increasingly be sustained by contract research and continuous government grants. Even if Newman's high ideals were attenuated, the growth of the research function within universities did not displace the importance of teaching. However, it did frequently bring research into conflict with it. In addition, a new conflict emerged between 'external' pressures to make education reflect the demands of employment and vocational training and the 'internal' orientation of academics toward the reproduction of disciplines and recruitment to postgraduate programmes.[5]

Kerr's arguments coincided with the expansion of higher education and with the enrolment of a generation of students, many of whom were the first in their families to attend universities. His wider arguments about the university were quickly overtaken by a wave of student and faculty radicalism that attacked his acceptance that one of its roles was engagement with the corporate economy. His critics perceived a different role for the university, as part of the democratization of public life against its increasing domination by corporate interests. In this way, an older idea of the university as a community engaged with fundamental issues of culture and public life was also articulated, if only briefly, and frequently with a radical and combative tone.

Kerr's account of the modern university was prescient. The 'students for democracy' of the 1960s and 1970s have become recast as consumers of education and investors in their own human capital (even if the student occupations and protests that have accompanied the current government's plans have provided an echo of those past concerns).[6] Kerr's book has been republished four times, when he returned to his original themes with the benefit of hindsight. Each new edition shows him becoming progressively less sanguine and more concerned about the future. He came to suggest that some of the functions of the multiversity might atrophy and that a more restricted funding environment (associated in his local context with relatively poor productivity growth in the US economy and competing demands for public funds) would increase competition among universities, a competition in which privately funded universities might benefit over those still reliant on some public funding.[7]

Universities, Kerr argued, would also confront resistance to spending on activities other than those that could be justified in terms of their contribution to health and medicine, economic growth or the development of the military-industrial complex, all of which could command support in the electoral politics of public spending. There would be a decline, he suggested, in the humanities and most social sciences, except that they functioned in support of these 'big three' topics, and there would be a decline in the concern with equalities and the social mission of the university. Each of these developments, then, represents a potential 'pathology' of the modern university, especially of the research university. In this respect, then, for Kerr, the health of a university cannot be judged simply by its financial position or place within global rank orders, but by the extent to which it manages the tensions among its different purposes.

Despite the fact that nearly all university vice-chancellors and senior administrators, and civil servants involved in higher education, have read Kerr's account of the multiversity, it is hard to resist the conclusion that current policies for higher education in the UK reinforce the very pathologies that Kerr described. For example, the current emphasis is upon the 'big three' topics and research is to be driven by a funding agenda that emphasizes the importance of 'impact' over the short and medium term. Public funding for teaching in the arts, humanities and social sciences has been withdrawn, to be retained only for 'priority' subjects (themselves defined by reference to the 'big three'). Otherwise, the direction of university teaching and research is to be determined by the market, to be driven by student choices in the light of their (necessarily partial and problematic) knowledge of the differential returns to education from different subjects and universities. These differential returns are expected to be matched by differential fees, with 'for-profit' providers and further education colleges entering to undercut fees at the lower end. Education to degree level will no longer presuppose a university education, a return to the situation that prevailed prior to the Robbins Report.

The introduction of student fees does not create a system that is sustainable for the future. With fees at £6,000, students will pay more for courses that will receive fewer resources than they do under the system of funding that is being replaced. With fees at £9,000, and set to rise higher in the future, students will be asked to pay high fees for the privilege of attending a selective university with the likely consequence that a portion of those fees (especially when fees rise further) will be used to fund research. The conflict between teaching and research that Kerr argued to be characteristic of the research university is set to continue. Indeed, it is now made general to the system, despite the emphasis on placing the 'student at the centre', with teaching universities starved of resources (including access to research funding) and research universities privileging research over teaching. Insofar as students are attracted by the 'brand', they will be encouraged to seek a place at a 'selective' university regardless of its teaching quality or of the proportion of the fees that they bring being devoted to teaching.

Finally, the introduction of higher, differentiated student fees exacerbates issues of equality of access and undermines the social mission of universities in terms of the democratization of higher education. Indeed, the differentiation of universities is likely to reinforce current tendencies where most students are from middle-class backgrounds, with low participation from students from working-class backgrounds. Moreover, as Roberts (2010) has suggested, the differentiation of types of universities is likely to create a division between students from the upper middle class and those from the middle class, with the former concentrated in 'selective' universities.[8]

Writing in 1931 in his book on *Equality*, R.H. Tawney observed that the English make a 'religion of inequality' and, further, that they seem to 'like to be governed by Etonians' (1964 [1931]). Our new political

governing caste has certainly made the market its article of faith,[9] with
the cynical consequence that only those able to attend 'elite institutions'
will have the advantage of enjoying the wider purposes of education
that have previously sustained our system of public universities. If, as
Newfield argues (2008), the attack upon the public university is an attack
upon the middle class – that is, the wider population (including women
and ethnic minorities) brought into universities following the expansion
of mass higher education and, thus challenging higher education as a
form of cultural capital appropriate for the privileged few – then the
reforms currently being enacted in England represent that attack in its
pure form. It is not the consequence of the atrophy of public funding and
various kinds of populist tax revolts as skirmishes within the cultural
wars. It is systematic government policy designed to dismantle fifty years
of educational policy that sought to establish education as a social right.

The idea of the public

For the most part, Kerr was concerned to provide sociological description
rather than philosophical insight. In these terms, there can be no way
back from the multiversity to an earlier idea of the university, nor can the
public university be defended by reference to principles that derive from
a status order with which it is now in conflict. However, it is important
to acknowledge that the necessary public functions of the university are
part of the same processes of development that seem now to be calling
them into question. To argue for the public university and its social
mission is not to look back to a 'golden age' of the university before mass
higher education, but to embrace the very principles associated with the
development of mass higher education.

For Kerr, the atrophy of the public functions of the university
represents a potential crisis in the 'advancement of trained intelligence'
(2001 [1995]) and this, for him, is what the future requires, not nostalgia
for a (mispresented) past. Kerr derives the phrase from Alfred North
Whitehead, but a similar term is used by the American pragmatist
philosopher, John Dewey, in his idea of 'collective intelligence'. I suggest
that it is through the idea of the public university as an instrument for
'collective intelligence' that we can begin to understand its fundamental
role for culture and for public life. In what remains of this chapter, I shall
address this requirement in terms of the idea of the 'public' and how its

interests may be served by the university.

First, I want to examine the rhetoric of the 'public' and its 'interests', as it functions in the justifications of current policies, especially those associated with the 'Big Society' and the opposition to 'Big Government'. The public is variously invoked as having an interest in the reduction of the fiscal deficit, an interest in greater choice and an interest in the efficient delivery of services. In this way, the public is identified as an aggregate of private individuals and government is tasked with representing its interests. The public interest, conceived in this way, is set against a tendency of groups to exert a form of collective power to maintain services to their own, private benefit. In this way, 'producers' of services are set against 'consumers' and the way to prevent their 'monopolistic' appropriation is via a mechanism that serves their interests directly, that of the market.

Indeed, the problem of 'collectivities' is extended to government itself, which, apparently, must represent the public against its own tendency to appropriate decision-making. On its website, the Cabinet Office states that, 'The Big Society is about helping people to come together to improve their own lives. It's about putting more power in people's hands – a massive transfer of power from Whitehall to local communities.'[10] One of the weaknesses of this rhetoric is that the transfer is to communities in which markets also operate. At best, it represents the self-organizing community as the solution to 'market failure'.[11] However, the market is also represented as putting more power in people's hands and so the policies that promote the 'Big Society' are simultaneously engaged with the promotion of the market. What is missing is any understanding that the market is itself 'anti-social', bringing about the 'disorganization' of the community whose empowerment is being sought. The 'Big Society' is countered to the 'Big State', but there is no equivalent analysis of the role of the market.

The first usage of the term 'Big Society' – or its analogue, the 'Great Society' – occurs in a speech by President Woodrow Wilson in 1913. He uses it to describe the shift from a society of individuals to a society where the relation among individuals was mediated by large-scale organizations, primarily those of the corporate economy. This theme was taken up by Graham Wallas in a book, *The Great Society* (1936), but which he describes in a preface as having a gestation back in 1910 and to discussions with the American political theorist, Walter Lippmann. I do not want to get into the nature of Wallas' argument for a new social psychology, but Lippmann's (1925) contribution to the debate is crucial, since it forms the context of John Dewey's intervention.

Essentially, the core of Lippmann's argument is that increased social complexity undermines the possibility of democracy approximating the forms endorsed by standard liberal accounts of representative democracy. The public, for Lippmann, is increasingly ill-equipped to make the sort of judgements attributed to it within democratic theory. He argues that the public is a 'phantom category' (that is, something that functioned only in theories of democracy and had little real substance). For Lippmann, what Dewey came to call the 'eclipse of the public' is a necessary consequence of the complexity of modern societies that increasingly required organized expertise of various kinds. In consequence, 'expert opinion' would replace 'public opinion' and democracy would necessarily be attenuated. Lippmann anticipated that expert opinion would operate in conjunction with the state and economic corporations and, in effect, would be 'co-produced' by them. These are ideas about the relation between knowledge and public policy that continue to determine the thinking of research councils and government, especially in the UK in terms of the 'impact agenda' (Research Councils UK n.d.).

Dewey's book, *The Public and Its Problems* (1927), is a riposte to Lippmann. However, he also noted that the 'eclipse of the public' is prefigured in the very idea of the market economy in which decisions by (consumer) sovereign individuals are perceived to be efficiently aggregated through impersonal market exchanges. This is held to be in contrast to their inefficient aggregation by collective political decision-making through the agency of the state. In other words, according to Dewey, the idea of a political realm in which the public expresses its democratic will is already severely compromised by the liberal distrust of 'group', or collective, actions and the idea that it is only the market that can properly express the general interest.

Dewey proposes to rescue the public from its eclipse by market and expert opinion by a radical refocusing of political philosophy, not as a *theory of the state* and its forms, but as a *theory of the public* and of the relation of institutional forms to the public, with the university as one crucial institutional form. He does so through an account of the 'social self', which he contrasts with the 'liberal self', as expressed in economics and political theory (in this way, also indicating the normative assumptions in the liberal idea of instrumental knowledge).

Dewey begins from the argument that the individual is necessarily a social being involved in 'associative life', and that this is true of what are conventionally regarded as private actions as well as of public actions.[12] For Dewey, individuals form associations, but they are also formed by associations. At the same time, the multiplicity of associations and their interconnected actions have consequences. In all of this, Dewey's idea of a 'public', and of the several nature of 'publics', is crucial. It contains a strong idea of democracy associated with participation and dialogue, but does not deny that there will be functionally differentiated publics, whose articulation will be at issue. The key to his definition of a public is contained in the idea of action in the world having effects and consequences that are ramified and impact upon others who are not the initiators of the action. Essentially, all action is associative action, but a public is brought into being in consequence of being indirectly and seriously affected by those actions of others. His analysis of the problem of modern democracy, then, is concerned with the imbalance in the development of associations and the proliferation of problems in areas where the public cannot properly defend itself.

This immediately raises the issue of the state as the representative of the 'public'. It is the point at which Dewey shifts gear to argue that the wider idea of a public can achieve a level of generality that requires organization and personnel to express it. This is the idea of a state, understood as a set of public authorities. Thus, Dewey proposes that, 'the lasting, extensive and serious consequences of associated activity bring into existence a public. In itself it is unorganized and formless. By means of officials and their special powers it becomes a state. A public articulated and operating through representative officers is the state; there is no state without a government, but also there is none without the public' (1927: 67).

Dewey by no means suggests that these developments mean that a state necessarily will act in the public interest – power can be accrued, authority can be exercised despotically and, indeed, the personnel of government can act on their own private or other special interests. The fundamental point, however, is that the state takes its meaning from the idea of a public and its interests, and that this is conceived as a dynamic thing. This means that, for Dewey, not only associations external to the state, but the state itself and its modes of organization are subject to change and revision in the light of other changes in the development of associative life. In other words, although the state exists in relation to the problems of associative, social life that create a public, its own forms and modes of organization may come to constitute a problem for the expression of that public, although, paradoxically, that is its *raison d'être*. So far, then, Dewey is expressing ideas that fit with concerns recently expressed under the idea of the 'Big Society'.

However, Dewey has as his target two pathologies. The first *sets the state against the public*, and is attributed to liberal individualism and its argument for the minimum state. The second is attributed to the conditions of modern corporate capitalism in which there appears to be an *'eclipse of the public'* brought about by the dominance of corporate interests over the state. Dewey argues that the first undermines the individual as surely as it seeks to set the individual free. This is because the ruling idea of liberalism is that of the individual free of associations, which is linked with the idea of the 'naturalness' of economic laws (embodied in market exchanges). It is precisely the ideology of liberal individualism, according to Dewey, that suggests that the market can replace the state as the regulator of social life, but leaves the individual vulnerable to the outcomes of the market.

However, according to Dewey, this doctrine emerged just as the idea of an 'individual' free of associations was being rendered untenable by the very developments of corporate capitalism with which it was linked. Thus, Dewey says that, '"the individual", about which the new philosophy centred itself, was in process of complete submergence in fact at the very time in which he was being elevated on high in theory' (1927: 96). The ideology which operates in the name of the individual, then, serves to undermine the very protection of the individual from egoistic, corporate associations that were themselves the very antithesis of the doctrine being espoused.

For Dewey, what is necessary for the proper expression of the public and for democracy is a 'Great Community'. Without it, the 'Big Society' involves nothing more than state-supported corporate interests, together with partial and ad hoc responses. In contrast, Dewey writes of democracy in the 'Great Community' that:

> From the standpoint of the individual, it consists in having a responsible share according to capacity in forming and directing the activities of the groups to which one belongs and in participating according to need in the values which the groups sustain. From the standpoint of the groups, it demands liberation of the potentialities of members of a group in harmony with the interests and goods which are in common. Since every individual is a member of many groups this specification cannot be fulfilled except

when different groups interact flexibly and fully in connections with other groups. (1927: 147)[13]

The university and the public

What does all of this have to do with the modern university? Dewey was also writing at the birth of the 'multiversity'. Knowledge production and professional services were coming increasingly to be university-based, and, at the same time, the university was becoming increasingly involved in the corporate economy with the commodification of research. Yet, Dewey wishes to argue that the university has a necessary role for democracy and in facilitating the Great Community.

The key issue is whether the complexity attributed to modern society and the problems it poses for a democratic public can be answered by the role of 'experts'. Quite apart from the undemocratic implications of the argument, Dewey also challenges it on sociological grounds. In contemporary discussions of the impact of research, much is made of the engagement with users and the development of 'pathways to impact' in which research is 'co-produced' with users or beneficiaries of it (Research Councils UK n.d.). However, this takes the structure of associations as given, when the problem of publics is always the problem of the consequences of associated actions for others. How are the 'publics' affected in the knowledge process to be protected and brought into a responsible share in the direction of activities? 'Co-production' is necessarily based upon forms of inclusion and exclusion (Jasanoff 2004). On Dewey's analysis, this is not something that can be left to government. Indeed, this is evident in the current government's management of the fiscal deficit, which is having very significant and differential consequences, with the very wealthy increasing their share and those most disadvantaged bearing a disproportionate burden, an outcome justified by reference to the 'market'.[14]

While the operation of economic interests can operate unseen, precisely because of the formal separation of economic and political institutions typical of modern capitalism, the application of expert knowledge must necessarily take place in front of the public. Where the argument about the role of experts depends upon the idea that the public is unable to judge complex matters, it remains the case that they will be able to judge the pretensions of experts. Moreover, they are likely to be vulnerable to populist mobilizations by the very interests that expert opinion is being called upon to moderate. Thus, Dewey writes that, 'rule by an economic class may be disguised from the masses; rule by experts could not be covered up. It could only be made to work only if the intellectuals became the willing tools of big economic interests. Otherwise they would have to ally themselves with the masses, and that implies, once more, a share in government by the latter' (1927: 206). As soon as 'expertise' is defined in terms of the instrumentalization of knowledge, there arises the problem that it is aligned with interests and, thereby, a problem of trust.

What is prescient is Dewey's concern with the problem of expert publics and their relation to wider publics. As expertise is increasingly co-produced, so what seems to be attenuated is the role of the wider public. In a context where risks of concentrated activities – whether of nuclear power production or carbon-hungry economic profit-seeking, to give just two examples – are also seen to be widely (indeed, globally) distributed, those that are affected are displaced from participation in decisions about them. At the same time, the nature of democracy is that wider public opinions can be made to count in elections and are subject to populist influence by advertising and by mass media, precisely as Dewey set out. It is hard to resist Turner's conclusion that the problem of expertise is one of the defining problems of modern democracy (Turner 2003). And if that is so, the answer necessarily entails a university functioning for the public. For Dewey, the significance of expert knowledge is how it can facilitate public debate, not government and corporate decision-making independently of the participation of the wider public. The increasingly embedded character of expert knowledge within corporations and government serves to de-legitimate expertise precisely by these forms of associations. It is necessarily part of the 'eclipse of the public'. As Dewey puts it, 'the essential need ... is the improvement of the methods and conditions of debate, discussion and persuasion. That is *the* problem of the public' (1927: 208).

If the improvement of debate, discussion and persuasion is *the* problem, then the university is necessarily part of the answer. But, it is only part of the answer *if it is at the service of the public*. A university at the service of the public, in Dewey's sense, is a university that should properly be regarded as a public university. This would not be the only function of a university, but it is a necessary function and it is one that would place social justice at its heart. Anything less and the university is just another private corporation in which a corporate economy has become a corporate society. The university would finally have given up any pretension to a social mission other than being at service to whoever paid.

2

Redefining the Public University: Global and National Contexts

Michael Burawoy

The university is in crisis, almost everywhere. In the broadest terms, the university's position as simultaneously inside and outside society – as both a participant in and an observer of society (always precarious) – has been eroded. With the exception of a few hold-outs the ivory tower has gone. We can no longer hold a position of splendid isolation. We can think of the era that has disappeared as the 'Golden Age of the University', but in reality it was a fool's paradise that simply could not last. Today, the academy has no option but to engage with the wider society; the question is how, and on whose terms? In this chapter, I examine the twin pressures of regulation and commodification to which the university is subject, propose a vision of the public university, and position that vision within different national contexts and then within a global context before concluding with the assertion of critical engagement and deliberative democracy as central to a redefined public university.

Market and regulatory models

We face enormous pressures of instrumentalization, turning the university into a means for someone else's end. These pressures come in two forms – commodification and regulation. I teach at the University of California, which had been one of the shining examples of public education in the world. In 2009 it was hit with a 25 per cent cut in public funding. This was a sizeable chunk of money. The university has never faced such a financial crisis since the Depression in the 1930s and it was forced to take correspondingly drastic steps – laying off large numbers of non-academic staff, putting pressure on already outsourced low-paid service workers, furloughing academics that included many world-renowned figures, introducing management consultants to cut costs and increase efficiency. Most significantly it involved a 30 per cent increase in student fees, so that they now rise to over $10,000 a year, but still only a quarter of the price of the best private universities. At the same time, the university is seeking to increase the proportion of students from out of state as these pay substantially more than those from in-state. There has been talk of introducing distance learning and even shortening the time taken for a degree.

These are drastic measures indeed, and the antithesis of the California Master Plan for Higher Education, Clark Kerr's vision of free higher education for all who desired it, orchestrated through a system that integrated two-year community colleges, the state system of higher education and then, at its pinnacle, the University of California, crowned by its jewel of the Berkeley Campus. All this is undergoing major transformation as each campus scrambles for ways to make up the budget deficit. In the end the elite universities will survive, but at the expense of the non-elite parts of the system where degradation of conditions for educators and educated is far more precipitous.

It has not been an overnight process. The state has been withdrawing funds from higher education for over three decades so that before these recent cuts it supplied only about 30 per cent of the university's budget. So a 25 per cent reduction in state-funding is more like a 7 per cent cut in the university's budget – still a sizeable proportion. The cuts began in the 1980s with the new era of marketization. Reflecting that broader shift was a change in how society viewed intellectual property rights, a change marked by the 1980 Bayh–Dole legislation on patents for intellectual property arising from federal government-funded research. Before then, patenting was seen as an infringement of the market. Knowledge was a public good that should be available to all and no one should have a monopoly access to its revenues. That changed and today a patenting mania invites expanding industry/university collaboration, including some $500 million from BP for research on non-fossil fuels at Berkeley (in partnership with the University of Illinois, Urbana-Champaign). As leading public universities cashed in on their research so the government saw less need to pour funds into higher education, which only further intensified the commercialization of knowledge, with devastating implications for those disciplines that could not convert their knowledge into tangible assets. They were told to find alumni or corporate donors to support their enterprise (see Bok 2003; Kirp 2003).

As a result, the university came to look more and more like a corporation, and its managerial ranks expanded rapidly. Akos Rona-Tas has calculated that, at the University of California between 1994 and 2009, the ratio of senior managers to ladder-ranked faculty has risen from 3:7 to 1:1, and the salary structure has been distorted accordingly.[1] The President of the university now expects to earn the equivalent of a corporate executive salary – he actually earns in excess of $800,000, which is twice the salary of the President of the country. All managerial and administrative salaries are stretched accordingly, and salaries within the university become ever more unequal, varying with the marketability of the associated knowledge and the credentials they produce. At every level inequality runs amok – between universities and within universities, between schools and within schools, between disciplines and within disciplines, between departments and within departments. Those who cannot sell their research initiate new ways of selling their teaching through online services that lead to dilution and lower costs of instruction.

At the global level we are also getting differentiation at the behest of international ranking systems – Times Higher Education (once with QS, now working with Thomson Reuters) or Shanghai Jiao Tong – indicating the 'world class' universities where private investments are likely to yield the greatest returns. Markets have invaded every dimension of the university, and its 'autonomy' now means only that it can choose the way to tackle budget deficits, whether through restructuring its faculties, employing temporary instructors, outsourcing service work, raising student fees, moving to distance learning, etc.[2]

This is the commodification model; now let me turn to the second model – the regulation model. The source of this model, we might say, was the Thatcher regime in the UK. Here the strategy is not to commodify the production of knowledge (or at least not immediately), that is, not to bring the public university into the market, but instead to make it more efficient, more productive and more accountable by more direct means. The Thatcher regime introduced the notorious Research Assessment Exercise (RAE) into British higher education – an elaborate scheme of evaluation based on faculty research output as measured by publications. A complex incentive scheme was introduced, with the collaboration of the universities, to simulate market competition but in reality it looked more like Soviet planning.[3] Just as the Soviet planners had to decide how to measure the output of their factories, how to develop measures of plan fulfilment, so now universities have to develop elaborate indices of output, KPIs (key performance indicators), reducing research to publications, and publications to refereed journals, and refereed journals to their impact factors. Just as Soviet planning produced absurd distortions, heating that could not be switched off, shoes that were supposed to suit everyone, tractors that were too heavy because targets were in tons or glass that was too thick because targets were in volume, so now the monitoring of higher education is replete with parallel distortions that obstruct production (research), dissemination (publication) and transmission (teaching) of knowledge.

British higher education has developed an elaborate auditing culture that has led academics to devote themselves to gaming the system, distorting their output – such as publishing essentially the same article in different outlets – while devaluing books, and creating and attracting academic celebrities to boost RAE ratings. Perhaps the most debilitating consequence has been the shortening of the time horizons of research, so that it becomes ever more superficial. This Soviet model has been exported from Britain to Europe with the Bologna Process that homogenizes and dilutes higher education across countries, all in the name of transferability of knowledge and mobility of students, making the university a tool rather than a motor of the knowledge economy.

The Soviet or regulation model is especially applicable, therefore, to those states that want to hold on to public higher education, but seek to rationalize it rather than privatize it. What is happening today, however, is more sinister – rationalization as a vehicle for effective commodification. As fiscal austerity grips Britain, and indeed much of Europe, free and open access to universities becomes a luxury so that the auditing system is now deployed against those disciplines, such as philosophy or sociology, which are least profitable. State subsidies per student are not only cut but are made to vary by discipline. Those with the lowest selling price – Band D – are most at risk. As we saw in the Soviet Union, planning turned to shock therapy, which proved to be all shock and no therapy. We should be aware of what has happened in Russia. Its universities became commercial operations – charging market rates for degrees in different disciplines, selling diplomas to the highest bidders, renting out real estate on the one side and buying academic labour at ever lower prices under ever-worsening conditions on the other. Education and research are afterthoughts, sustained in a few pockets of protected higher education. With the destruction of the old order the market rules unopposed. Alexander Bikbov (Bikbov 2010) rightly asks whether the Russian university is the future of the world.

An alternative framing

Our two models – commodification and regulation – are ideal typical tendencies which combine in different ways according to place and time. Is there an alternative model which we may use as a reference to evaluate these two, yet point towards other possibilities? How shall we think of the university today in the light of these two tendencies? Each model raises its own question about the nature of the production of knowledge and thus the university. Commodification of knowledge leads to production for the highest bidder, and that often means that scholars are led out of the university to sell their skills to some policy client. In many parts of the world, such as Africa and the Middle East, it has spelled the end of the university as we know it, as the best scholars leave for more rewarding employers who seek short-term returns on poorly conducted research. Commodification raises the question of *knowledge for whom?* Are we producing knowledge for ourselves as a community of scholars or for a world beyond the academy? In reality each needs the other, there can be no serious knowledge of an applied character without careful development of knowledge within scientific research programmes. There is no short-circuiting of knowledge production. Still, knowledge for its own sake – pure knowledge – also needs to be inspired by questions and issues beyond the university.

If commodification raises the question of knowledge for whom, regulation raises the question of knowledge for what? All the mechanisms of regulation, whether through ranking systems or through standardization, repress the reason for producing knowledge. Here we have to ask whether knowledge is produced as a means to a given end – an end defined by someone else, whether this be a policy client or a research programme – or whether knowledge should be concerned with a discussion of ends themselves, whether this be a discussion among academics about the direction of scientific knowledge or between academics and wider publics as to the goals of society more broadly. The first type of knowledge I call *instrumental knowledge* as it is concerned with orienting means to ends, while the second type of knowledge

I call *reflexive knowledge* as it is concerned with dialogue about values themselves. It is the reflexive knowledge that is being sacrificed by the instrumentalization of the university.

In problematizing both commodification and regulation we have posed two sets of questions, knowledge for whom and knowledge for what, that give us Table 2.1.[4]

	AUTONOMY Academic Audience	HETERONOMY Extra-Academic Audience
Instrumental knowledge	PROFESSIONAL	POLICY
Reflexive knowledge	CRITICAL	PUBLIC

Table 2.1   The functions of the public university

This vision of the public university recognizes four functions of the university. At the heart is professional knowledge, the knowledge produced in research programmes defined in the academic world evaluated by fellow academics. The knowledge can then be applied to the world beyond in the policy realm, but recognizes the interdependence of the two knowledges. You cannot short circuit the academic world and produce meaningful and durable knowledge on demand by clients. But a dialogic relation between clients with their problems can generate new and interesting challenges for research programmes.

Sustaining the autonomy of professional knowledge is the role of what I have called critical knowledge that depends on the existence of a community of scholars. Critical knowledge is the conscience of the community; it insists on maintaining the conditions of professional knowledge that it does not veer off into world of its own. It creates a community of discourse that transcends disciplines. Finally, public knowledge is the conversation between sociologists and wider publics about the broad direction of society and the consequences that might follow. Just as there is an interdependence of professional and policy knowledge, so the same is true of critical and public knowledge – each infuses others with a discussion of the values recognized by society.

Against the instrumentalization, both regulation and commodification, of knowledge the survival of the university depends on the reassertion of reflexive knowledge, which means the university community has to develop a collective conscience but also has to counter policy definitions of the worth of knowledge and elaborate the longer term interests, building society in the university and the university in society.

In other words, what I am redefining as the *public university* gives weight to each of the four types of knowledge, requires them to be in dialogue with each other and recognizes their interdependence, even as they are in an antagonistic relation.[5] Each knowledge depends upon the other three. Thus, public knowledge requires the value discussions inspired by critical knowledge and the scientific work of professionals, but also draws on the policy context. Professional knowledge shrivels up if it does not enter into dialogue with the policy world, if its foundations are not subject to interrogation from critical knowledge and if it does not translate itself into public debates about the direction of society. Policy knowledge becomes captive of its clients, and thus more ideology than science, if it loses touch with public debate, with the accumulation of knowledge in research programmes, and with the organized scepticism that comes from critical engagement. Critical knowledge, itself, depends on having the professional and policy worlds to interrogate, but also gains much of its energy from the public debates to which it also contributes.[6]

The balance among these knowledges certainly will vary from discipline to discipline within the university. The hard sciences emphasize the instrumental moment of knowledge, varying in their emphasis on professional as opposed to policy knowledge, but that is not say they do not also have a reflexive moment, engaging in discussion of the implications of their science for the wider society. The humanities may be oriented toward the reflexive dimension but that is not to say that they too do not have autonomous paradigms of investigation and exploration and the more they influence the foundations of policy considerations the better. The social sciences, one might say, form the pivot around which the four knowledges revolve since their central task is to understand the relation between instrumental and reflexive knowledge as well as to negotiate academic and extra-academic knowledge. The social sciences have a key mediating role to play within and without the university.

We might also extend this framework to teaching, recognizing that pedagogy also comes in four modes: professional teaching that imparts to students the accumulated body of knowledge that defines a discipline or area of study; policy teaching that is more like vocational education, the application of knowledge to a particular occupation; critical teaching that examines the foundations of knowledge and its existence; and teaching as public engagement. The latter regards students not as empty vessels, but as members of a public with their own interests and experiences that are elaborated through pedagogical dialogue based in different disciplines. Again, we can say there is an elective affinity between certain disciplines and the articulation of these different ways of teaching.

The University in the national context

Combining all four forms of knowledge, the public university is the ideal type response to the regulation and commodification models. But how realistic is it? What are the pressures on the university that make it sustainable or not? We must now place this model in a national context to see how it survives. In order to do that I break down the four realms of knowledge into an inner and outer zone – the inner zone is necessary to sustain the integrity of the university while the outer region mediates the impact of the world beyond.

As budget crises hit the university so the tendency is to seek out short-term economic gain through the sale of knowledge, whether this be in the form of increasing student fees, individual consultancies or collaborations with clients. In each case the result can be subjugation to the interest of the client. Whether it be subservience to capital or the dictatorship of student desires, the commodification of knowledge undermines its integrity. We can call this a *sponsorship* model of policy research in which the initiative comes from without. But we cannot reduce policy science to sponsorship; the academic world has its say too. It is, in other words, a negotiated relation in which sponsorship is but one end of a continuum that has *advocacy* at the other end. In the latter model academics take the initiative in proposing policies for clients, recognizing their interests as framing the problems to be solved but not surrendering their independence. Thus, Douglas Massey's view of immigration to the United States adopts the interests of the state in reducing the flow of undocumented immigration and shows how reinforcing borders actually locks immigrants into the United States, only exacerbating the problem (Massey 2006). The best and most original policy initiatives come from academics who are allowed to make proposals of their own, proposals often critical of government policy. It is not enough to be critical of sponsored research: we have to counter with reservoirs of advocacy research, but that requires continual contact with professional knowledge. Just as the capturing of policy science threatens the integrity of the university, so can the regulation of professional knowledge. We can distinguish between *formal rationality* that secures the institutional prerequisites – such as peer review, competitive production of knowledge, hierarchies of publication outlets – and *substantive rationality* that is the expansion (or contraction) of research programme-based attempted solutions of anomalies and contradictions. The danger is that formal rationality, rather than protecting, undermines substantive rationality through the development of extraneous measures of 'excellence' that then become the basis of novel incentive systems as in the UK's Research Assessment Exercise. In pursuit of 'world-class university' status, the university is removed from its ties to national and local issues. We will have more to say about this below when we introduce the global context.

The ascendancy of formal rationality in the regulation model feeds into the commercialization of the commodification model, making critical engagement all the more important. But here we have a different tension: between disciplinary and interdisciplinary criticisms. Interdisciplinarity presupposes disciplinary research with its distinctive array of interconnected assumptions, methodologies, theoretical frameworks and guiding questions. New disciplines may emerge, but there is no eliminating of disciplines for all their potential narrowing of perspectives. That is how knowledge progresses – through disciplinary frameworks, ever more necessary to organize and make sense of the exponential growth in information. Still, these frameworks must be subject to continual criticism and that is the role of critical debate and the interrogation of fundamentals, not least the distortion of knowledge by an extraneous regulatory system, by the accentuation of formal rationality. It is critical knowledge that provides the corrective, calling attention to the underlying goals and values of any given research programme. Moreover, that critical knowledge is often inspired by ideas drawn from other disciplines, and even transdisciplinary thought. While dialogue with other disciplines can inspire critique, the danger is that it threatens to substitute itself for disciplinary development as in some expressions of poststructuralism that seek to abolish the very project of warranted knowledge.

Just as professional knowledge can be subverted from without

Figure 2.1 The matrix of knowledge in its national context

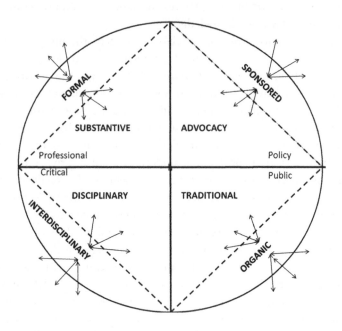

through formal rationalization and from within by devotion to the sustenance of regressive research programmes, so critical knowledge can become dogmatic and irrelevant if it loses touch with its disciplinary heritage and public issues. Public engagement holds professional and critical knowledge accountable to lay audiences. It does so in two ways. On the one hand there is the mediated dialogue with publics – what I call public knowledge of a *traditional* kind – that involves the generation of public debate through various forms of journalism and other media outlets. Audiences are addressed from on-high without entering into direct relations with publics, the opposite of what I call public knowledge of an *organic* kind. The former tends to engage publics that are thin, broad, passive and mainstream while the latter is more likely to engage publics that are thick, narrow, active and oppositional. The danger with public knowledge of the organic kind is the same with sponsored policy science – the loss of autonomy. As British industrial sociologists found, when they got close to the labour movement, the dialogue turned into a relation of servitude, in effect to become policy scientists beholden to clients. It is important, therefore, for scholars organically connected to their publics to also retain their attachment to professional knowledge, often via traditional forms of public scholarship that disdain proximate connection to publics. Public scholarship of a traditional kind maintains its autonomy but at the expense of influence and so it can benefit from connection to the more organic forms of scholarship.

Different societies allow for different balances between inner and outer zones of the four types of knowledge. Thus, in the social sciences, the United States has often been hyper-professionalized, and this can distort the substantive rationalization of research programmes. The commodification of knowledge, however, puts enormous pressure on policy research and collaborations between science and industry, all of which will come at the expense of the disciplines that are concerned with critical and public knowledge – the humanities. In the Soviet Union the world of sponsored policy research prevailed at the cost of all the others, and this legacy actually shaped the post-Soviet terrain, with the continued focus on short-term dividends of policy research sponsored by politicians, government or corporations. By reaction it has generated pockets of universities, here and there, that are driven by the defensive affirmation of a critical knowledge, dismissive of the policy orientation and embracing the idea of the liberal university. Many of the developing countries – Brazil, India and South Africa – that have emerged from authoritarian or colonial regimes into some form of democracy with a vibrant public sphere take for granted that the university has a public moment and, indeed, it is in these countries that the university still plays a major public role, sometimes at the expense of the professional knowledge.

The two large countries that have so far seemed to have escaped the budgetary crisis, that have well-funded university systems, are Brazil and China. In the case of Brazil the legacy of the previous dictatorship's commitment to the advance of science continues and the state funds a network of outstanding federal universities that jealously guard their autonomy. Academics have resisted the imposition of external standards of professional evaluation. China continues to expand its funding of universities, believing that their contributions will motor economic growth. Indeed, the Shanghai Jiao Tong University ranking system, now deployed worldwide, was designed to evaluate the best Chinese universities against the top US universities. Funding is driven by the policy dimension, but in recognition of the importance of the development of professional knowledge and the training of ever greater numbers of university graduates.

The global context

The configuration of national university systems is shaped by and shapes its insertion into a global context. Again our two models of regulation and commodification reflect pressures operating at the global level. Regulation refers to the systems of global competition for places in international ranking systems. This entails nation-states applying pressure to universities to compete globally along a range of indices, but most fundamentally to publish scholarly papers in major international journals, to teach and research in English, making US or European societies the reference point for everything. This draws the best university faculties into the orbit of an international community but in so doing they lose contact with national issues. While this most obviously affects the social sciences and humanities, it can also affect the hard sciences in that the medical and engineering problems faced by a country in the Global South can be very different from those faced in the Global North.

Moreover, by making US universities the model of excellence, poorer countries pour their scarce resources into an unattainable and arguably inappropriate goal, enriching one or two universities while impoverishing the rest. In some cases it becomes a justification for having no substantial university at all so that the training of students, especially postgraduates, takes place abroad. Where higher education remains, there is an ever deeper polarization between the top universities hooked into international circuits and the poorer universities mired in service to the locality: cosmopolitanism through regulation at one pole, localism as provincialism at the other. Examples of this can be found in the Middle East with its elite universities, such as the American Universities of Beirut and Cairo, following international standards, teaching the children of the wealthy in English and ever more differentiated from massified national universities suffering under appalling conditions and teaching in Arabic. No less instructive is the situation in Israel where the top universities consider themselves an appendage of the United States, making the best US universities their reference point, while the non-elite and technical universities are responsive to the needs of the locality.[7]

The ranking of universities serves market forces seeking to invest in or collaborate with the most profitable centres of knowledge production. University administrations, threatened with budget cuts, use their ranking as world-class universities to attract corporate donors, fee-paying foreign students and so forth. In some countries, for example

Figure 2.2 The university in its global context

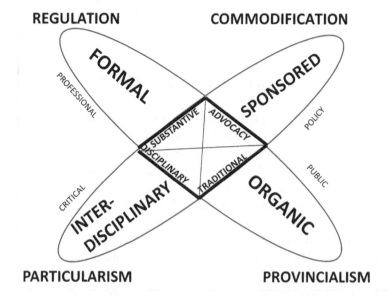

Turkey and South Korea, capital actually creates or buys up universities with the aim of producing centres of academic excellence. Owning a university becomes a mark of 'distinction' for corporate capital. As the market model becomes more important so corporations and governments begin to sponsor think-tanks and consultancies to engage directly with issues of immediate concern, drawing some of the best talent out of the universities. This is happening all over the world, not least in Europe, under the rubric of Mode-2 type knowledge (Nowotny, Scott and Gibbons 2001),[8] but its effects are especially pernicious in the Global South, where university employment does not provide a living wage and presumes multiple jobs. As faculty members depart for private-sector research organizations – and there too often to conduct quick and dirty research with short time horizons – so the university is no longer seen as a major source of knowledge production and suffers decline. This is the story across much of Africa (Mamdani 2007). Even in a country with as well-developed a system of higher education as South Africa universities have great difficulty holding on to their best talent, especially African talent which can find far more lucrative positions elsewhere. Market invasion involves the accentuation of sponsored policy research at one pole and a reactive critique at the other pole. Critical knowledge recoils against commodification and regulation, turning toward new inbred particularisms that draw on national traditions and altogether reject disciplinary thought.

What is to be done?

A vision for the public university, relevant to different national contexts and an overall global context, must counter the twin pressures of regulation and commodification to which the university is now subjected. Critical engagement and deliberative democracy are central to this vision of the redefined public university.

Global pressures, fostered by nation-states and international capital, giving priority to regulatory and commodification models, have led to the enormous divides within national systems of higher education, and between them. There is an ever greater concentration of resources in the top research universities in the Global North at the expense of the impoverishment of the majority universities there and also in the Global South. In all cases the reflexive moment is being outweighed by the instrumental moment.

The university is being pulled into regulatory and market systems that are destroying the very basis of its own precarious autonomy, its capacity to continue to produce and disseminate profound knowledge. The reflexive moment needs to be reasserted as a counterweight: the inner zones of the four knowledges – substantive professional knowledge, advocacy policy knowledge, traditional public knowledge and disciplinary critical knowledge – have to be brought into a systematic relation with one another. Each has to support the other in counteracting pressures on the outer zones – formal rationalization of professional knowledge, commercialization of policy knowledge, provincialization of public knowledge and particularistic critical knowledge.

Against the regulatory and market models we have to formulate alternative models of the university – two in particular. First, the university should be viewed as a *critical public sphere* in which there is indeed discussion among academics about the nature of the university and its place in society. The recent outpouring of books, discussions and blogs about the university suggests that there is a lively debate about the fate of the university, but it has to happen across disciplines. The humanities cannot confine their defence as repositories of wisdom for the education of responsible citizens – though they must do that – they have also to inject a critical and reflective moment into the discussion about the fate of the university. If the critical public sphere is one alternative model, the idea of *deliberative democracy* is the second. Here the university has to be at the centre of organizing public discussion about the direction of society. As the more conventional representatives of publics – trade unions, political parties, voluntary organizations, religious associations – are falling down on their public mission, the university has to take up its calling as the pivotal institution to orchestrate a deliberative democracy. Each nation has to find its own balance among these models of the university – regulatory, market, critical engagement, deliberative democracy – and the balance will look very different across the globe, but we have to get away from the idea of a single model for the university, a model not just based in the West, but in imitation of the richest universities in the West.

3

Open Universities: A Vision for the Public University in the Twenty-first Century

Nicola Miller and John Sabapathy

Something invaluable is about to be destroyed. British universities are on the verge of losing their freedom to pursue intellectual insight through teaching and research, a freedom that for the last century has been based on the state's willingness to rely on the commitment of universities to care for their disciplines, staff and students.[1] It is this freedom to let intellectual and educational values shape their work that has made British universities among the most successful in the world. Once that freedom has been lost, it will not be recovered quickly or easily, if it can be recovered at all.

Academic freedom and intellectual creativity in Britain have been under severe pressure for several decades, but they were finally given what is likely to prove a final blow by the cumulative effect of three decisions taken by the coalition government in December 2010. The first – a near tripling of tuition fees – received much publicity; the second – an 80 per cent cut in the teaching grant – attracted less attention; the third – a dramatic increase in the proportion of research funding that will be allocated to align with 'national strategic priorities' – has gone virtually unnoticed (Mandler 2011). Yet these last two shifts in particular will radically transform the dynamics of teaching provision and research in British universities in profoundly undesirable ways that reduce higher education to a commodity. This chapter argues that a far bolder and more compelling vision of what universities can and should be in the twenty-first century is needed.

Trapped in the panopticon

Before those three decisions were taken, university teachers and researchers retained at least some freedom to organize their teaching and research on the basis of educational and intellectual values. From now on, however, student choice will determine what they teach and civil servants will direct what they research. The university will soon become the panopticon, Jeremy Bentham's 'all-seeing, all-knowing' inspection-house, where teachers and thinkers are constantly surveyed and regulated in the name of efficiency. Given that our world is already so Benthamite, it is worth recalling the view of his assistant, John Stuart Mill, that in 'everything except abstract speculation', Bentham was an infant, his conceptions of human individuality the 'freaks of a pettish child' (Mill 1969: 115). Bentham's manifest failure to secure support for his panopticon prison in his own day is ironically and inversely matched by its extraordinary diffusion throughout modern society. Yet the last place Bentham would have wanted to see it implemented was the universities, which he believed should be places of free thinking, open to all without prejudice or favour.

The prospect of the panopticon is all the more appalling since this moment – between what universities could be and what they are about to be reduced to – is actually a time of extraordinary opportunity both for universities and society. The Browne Report (2010) sought a 'sustainable' future for Britain's universities: yet that report's vision is not so much sustainable as lacking in any ambition. The expansion of higher education begun in the 1980s was, regrettably, done on the cheap, which accounts for many of the problems universities currently face. However, a good deal of ground was made up during the 2000s and Britain now has a successful higher education sector, somewhat unwieldy and certainly not without its problems, but nonetheless attracting far more applications both from home and international students than it can accept. There is a tremendous appetite outside 'the academy' for deep and meaningful knowledge about the world – be that knowledge biological, astronomical, historical, literary or artistic. Look at the number of popular television or radio programmes on such subjects dependent on the academy for content and presenters. Inside universities, disciplinary self-questioning has stimulated imaginative new ways of teaching and researching many subjects. In our own field, history, scholarship is more diverse and richer today than it was fifty or even thirty years ago. Global developments, increasing transnational movements, have also opened up many more possibilities for exchanging knowledge and ideas, which have never been so rich for so many people, both internationally and within Britain – for all the legitimate concerns about social mobility.

But with these gains have come complexities to which both academics and politicians have struggled to find good responses – or even adequate ones. Many universities, like other institutions, are now strongly international in staff and students. It no longer makes sense for them to be seen as principally, or even mainly, the intellectual underwriters of their nation-states. Yet universities have to be located somewhere and should be sufficiently valuable to the communities in which they thrive to justify public funding. Of course, as has been persuasively argued by many people, universities can contribute a great deal to stimulating good citizenship. Yet citizenship has now acquired a global as well as a national dimension.

A further complexity lies in the discrediting of the Kantian model of 'universal reason' that underpinned the influential German university experiments of the later eighteenth and nineteenth centuries. It is now widely accepted that not only knowledge itself but also ways of knowing are profoundly shaped by the societies in which they are embedded. There are many more ways of knowing things than were dreamt of in Kant's philosophy, an awareness that is reflected in the fertile process of rethinking disciplines and their methods that has occurred over the last few decades. This is not a 'postmodern' fad. Teachers are reminded of its fundamental nature every time we encounter the bemusement of an international student – whether from China, France, Hungary or the United States of America – when faced with the peculiar demands of the British essay.

Losing the illusion of a universal model of intellectual life should be more of an opportunity than a constraint. It has undeniably caused disorientation in the universities of developed countries, but it certainly does not follow that we are condemned to fragmentation, isolation and inability to communicate. There is no sense in which universities are 'postmodern' factories for producing greater and greater uncertainty about more and more bodies of knowledge. Rather, in reducing the scope for baldly stating how things should be, new possibilities emerge for democratically debating how things could be. Not, 'This is the only way to know the world,' but 'Look what we learn from applying these approaches.'

If this seems disconcerting that is simply proof of how poorly academics and university administrators have struggled both to describe these facts and articulate some positive vision in relation to them. Politicians' and policy-makers' responses have been little better, being either crushingly instrumental in the most dispiriting way or simply incoherent. Recent governmental pronouncements on higher education's value have offered nothing more than an impoverishing sense of its contribution to UK GDP. As to incoherence, on the one hand the government has encouraged universities to 'compete globally in excellence', in the current jargon. On the other, it has jerked funding strings which yank universities towards more parochial priorities. The current pushmi-pullyu between government departments regarding foreign students' visas is just one example of this.

So it is worth stating a vision for the place of universities in society that we can support and want to fight for – specifically within a British society that is both part of our European community and of a more global civil society. The dust-storm surrounding the Browne Report has so far not provided any such compelling vision. The broader trend in university politics towards more and more concrete Benthamite panopticons is a drift towards a dystopia based on deluded fantasies of control and the mistaking of transparency for omniscience. It will produce an abdication of responsibility towards students, staff, society and the bodies of knowledge that universities have guaranteed for centuries. As language departments and science departments close across the country that effect is already demonstrably visible.

Exiting the panopticon: a new cultural contract for universities

Our vision, by contrast, is not, we believe, utopian, but one grounded in trust, responsibility and a more imaginative conception of what universities ought to be – indeed, what they already have the capacity to become. It is, above all, one in which intellectual and educational criteria are privileged before and beyond considerations of funding mechanisms, 'relevance' or the interests of self-perpetuating bureaucracies themselves. This is not because our vision disdains social 'utility', but because we believe that the best way to sustain the utility of higher education teaching and research in the longer term is to attend to intellectual and educational concerns first and foremost, not as a secondary requisite of other priorities. A vision is needed that attends to universities' responsibilities not just to society, but also to their students, their own staff, the disciplines they teach and their role as sites of systematic knowledge. Without such a vision, bright men and women will be less willing to teach and research there; bright young adults will want less to study there, and gain less from doing so; and society will benefit less and less, at levels not merely restricted to the narrowly economic. The vision we offer below is offered instead as a starting point for renegotiating a contract between university institutions, university staff, students, government and society. It is founded on a genuine commitment to responsibility.

Responsibility to students

What then might such a vision consist of? Some of its elements are exceptionally old. It would be facile to say that students arrive at university as children and leave as adults, but there is an important truth about the rite of passage that university provides for those young people who choose to attend. This is understood today, but often in absurdly narrow ways. It is not – contrary to the Confederation of British Industry's regular pronouncements – universities' function to produce men and women shrink-wrapped on exit for corporate workstations. It is universities' job to provide the space and the time in which teenagers can become adults.[2] This is partly a matter of technical training and instruction, equipping them with the ability to think critically in relation to various bodies of knowledge and disciplines.

It also means cultivating more global outlooks – specifically less 'Anglolexic' ones. In a global world, knowledge of other languages is a way of apprehending other cultures most immediately. Since successive governments of every hue have hollowed out foreign language teaching at schools, it seems important for universities to commit to rectifying this, insofar as they can. Universities should offer staff and students in all disciplines access to a range of languages, with the expectation that everyone will become familiar with at least one other modern language.

It is also a matter of socializing students more fundamentally, from classroom discussion to the range of extra-curricular activities for which universities can provide the space and resources. Adults need to leave universities consequently prepared to think constructively about the – now multiple – identities they must strive to integrate in the contemporary world. British graduates have been living in Britain and Europe under a host of confessional banners – and none – for a long time now. Those identities are not becoming less important. Furthermore, many students will go on to work in institutions that are large enough to have their own, potentially global, reach. Equipping students to respond to others' identities and to develop their own – responsibly and civilly – must be an important job for universities. For centuries universities have provided, for those qualified and willing to learn, one of the most important rites of passage available to young people. Those 'qualified' are no longer just those coming from the right diocese, as was partly true in of medieval universities. Religion and gender are, by and large, no longer inhibiting factors. Still, today, much remains to be done though in removing barriers to full participation by all those with the potential to benefit from degree-level education, irrespective of their social background.

The result of all these developments has been to place complex demands on universities and there is no doubt that they could support students better than they currently do in negotiating their identities.[3] This is to define a responsibility that universities have to society and to students themselves: that universities will provide them with safe and stimulating communities in which a large proportion of our most promising school-leavers can become thoughtful and engaged adults in our politics and our communities.

Responsibility to the integrity of knowledge

To achieve education to a worthwhile standard, and across the range of disciplines and subjects, society has a responsibility to protect the integrity of knowledge. Our disciplines, from Clio to Urania (History to Astronomy), have their claims. And without their mother, Memory herself, they are nothing. But memory is not enough. Knowledge that is not added to and reinterpreted in transmission is pickled not protected. The link between teaching and research is therefore not only vital to teaching energetically and ensuring the integrity of knowledge, it is also a way to ensure teachers themselves remain energized and engaged. There are many academics who will say that teaching first-year undergraduates is an important way to keep your feet on the ground, as well as the most stimulating teaching you can do. So this idea of responsibility to knowledge entails allowing for the claims of all those working on these subjects, both students *and* teachers, if we are to ensure their sustained quality.

Universities must therefore be enabled to preserve, develop and transmit knowledge, in all its forms. A commitment to that is a deep and sane measure of the quality of any society, whether 'big' or not. If we believe this to be true in Britain, then it should be obvious that relying on student choices at degree level as the mechanism to fund them is to abdicate any responsibilities to those disciplines. Students who have just left school often have little reliable idea of what they will turn out to be interested in. The proposed new arrangement means they will be far less likely ever to find out. Lowest common denominators will prevent it: faced with the need to predict income streams, heads of departments will be 'incentivized' to remove less predictable or unusual courses, course ranges will shrink, and impoverishing 'safety first' cultures will prevail, in all but the best-financed and largest universities. Disciplines, students, teachers and diversity will all suffer.

It should be equally obvious that if we have any responsible commitment to the integrity of our disciplines and its experts then the attention of researchers should follow their insights more, not less. That is not compatible with ideas for funding regimes that follow predetermined national strategies or themes. It makes complete sense for particular (passing but intense) concerns to receive particular (passing but intense) funding. It makes no sense to require all research to contribute to these concerns, not least because there is no way of knowing what may be 'relevant' concerns tomorrow. If all today's research has only attended to the concerns of the day, who will be equipped to research – or even recognize – the concerns of tomorrow? Genuine research is unpredictable. If any 'relevance' is foreseeable – rather than possible – then the researcher is either about to embark upon a piece of research that remains within the confines of what is already known or has already carried out the necessary research. To canonize 'relevance' as the only relevant criterion of deserving research is to encourage research that will date quickly.

Universities' responsibility to themselves

This responsibility to developing the integrity of knowledge turns out to be also a commitment to those who teach and research at universities. On this basis, people professionally dedicated to questioning, interpreting and making sense of the world would be given the responsibility to think, guided by the rigorous methods of their particular discipline, their ideas tested and debated by their peers. Some would pursue 'blue-skies research', others would seek to solve particular problems. Both approaches would accord each other respect in recognition of their mutual dependence.

But to produce both the sorts of responsibility described above requires that universities cultivate a further responsibility to themselves internally. This means finally abolishing the stagnant and disabling traces of the 'two cultures', arts and sciences, which do still persist in some universities. If universities are to live up to the vision we are developing here this is essential. Interdisciplinarity has been fashionable for some time now, but there remains much to be said for greater literacy – or numeracy – across disciplines. Sometimes this will be irrelevant, and problems will only be solved within robust and critical disciplinary perspectives. At other times we will need to step back from detailed consideration of our monitors, manuscripts or microscopes. Then it will be necessary to ask (say, in our own field) what should be the relationship between environmental history or forensic archaeology and the hard sciences of climate change if we wish to answer important questions about the historical relationship between human habitation, life chances and climatic change?

It is part of universities' responsibility to themselves in the long-run to create ways and spaces in which such work is made more, not less, likely. That is a challenge – we suspect – that not many universities have been successful in meeting. So universities need to develop critical consciences with respect to themselves. This is a responsibility they owe not only to their own development but also to those who underwrite them in society. Once again, 'student choice' will diminish a university's ability to discharge this responsibility, just in so far as universities are encouraged to be selective and no longer to embrace a broad range of subjects.

Responsibility to society

However, the point of developing such a critical conscience and consciousness is not that it should flourish only inside the academy as a way of proving our integrity. Such consciences need to feed back out into society.

The emphasis of many recent contributions to debates on higher education has been on the need for universities to be responsive to society. But it is a (partial) waste of the critical consciences we are advocating if they are only projected at those studying or working inside universities. This perspective has been encouraged by the view that universities should be the passive respondents to whatever 'society' wants them to respond. But the critical consciences that universities can develop should be prized also for their ability to instruct society about what universities have found to be important – and what universities think society should respond to (this is a corollary of the 'relevance' criticism above). Universities' insights will often – should often, perhaps – be contrary to what society thinks, or thinks it wants to hear. This is not a vision of a Platonic world of guardians who determine and arbitrate their societies. It is a vision in which responsiveness is not fatuously construed as the perquisite of those outside of universities to demand of those inside universities. It is also a vision in which the boundaries of who is inside and outside of universities needs to be renegotiated, quite dramatically in some respects. This needs to go beyond the basics of ensuring that universities are places in which 'the public' is welcome and can come in to comprehend (comprehensibly) what it is that those inside universities can see. The responsibility and the responsiveness must flow in both directions if some genuine new contract between universities is to be the basis of a functional, rather than a dysfunctional, relationship.

This vision is one of a virtuous circle. Universities enable children to become adults, a responsibility to society and to students. To fully discharge that responsibility to students they need to preserve, develop and transmit an ever-increasing body of knowledge that helps us understand and live in our world – a responsibility to those bodies of knowledge themselves. Yet this task is quite obviously not one of rote copying. In order to attract very bright and creative people the act of transmitting knowledge will also be an act of recreating knowledge. If those people are to be kept where they can educate children then they must be given the freedom to determine the priorities and interests of the research questions in their fields. To prescribe a priori what the development of knowledge must look like is by far the fastest route to ensure that what is one of Britain's great success stories will rapidly stagnate and produce ideological chaff, not intellectual wheat.

These responsibilities are to the disciplines and to the men and women who preserve and develop them – but they are also in the long term to the societies that can conceive of their value. To develop knowledge, though, universities must finally rid themselves of the hulks of the two cultures that still bureaucratically and architecturally litter their campuses. This is not to say that the overused term 'interdisciplinarity' is the salve for all ills, but it is to say that better, real, relationships between disciplines must be part of the basis for the integrated critical perspectives that we believe universities can offer. Finally, the vision described above is not one in which universities are passively 'responsive' to society, but instead actively contribute towards shaping and reshaping it. It is universities' final responsibility to challenge society itself. This vision is grounded in turning away from introverted panopticons, to more open universities, proud of the competencies, insights and value they embody and create within their disciplines and for society.

Towards open universities: from here to there

We are convinced that this vision of responsible universities is within reach, but conditions and expectations would have to change both in universities and in government, not to mention wider society. It is integral to the Prime Minister's vision of the Big Society that 'we've got to give professionals much more freedom'.[4] In universities the trend is in the opposite direction. The two under-examined changes discussed at the start of this chapter are cases in point. The removal of the block teaching grant institutionalizes a market-driven deregulation where knowledge will live and die depending on student markets – not the disciplinary importance of given courses. Conversely, the abandonment of the independent 'Haldane principle' establishes the basis for re-regulating research funding in line with governmental priorities. To institutionalize these two opposed impulses is to embed schizophrenia into the bodies of universities. The only thing they have in common is that they reduce the ability of academics to teach what matters and to research what is important.

More bureaucratically, the boxes that academics are required to tick keep on multiplying: teaching, research, publishing, knowledge transfer, public engagement, marketing, entrepreneurship. It becomes increasingly hard for academics to devote the time necessary to the slow, incremental work of teaching and research. If you turn universities into businesses you will not have universities any more. And the most successful businesses of the age – think of Google – operate on the basis that long-term productive commercial creativity is best secured by clearing space for research free from a concern with its immediate instrumentalization. How much truer should this be for universities? As we have said above, we do not advocate a return to the ivory tower, quite the opposite. Universities should become more open to society and to their local communities, but the quid pro quo must be that society becomes more open to universities and attaches more value to their intellectual and educational work. It is not only those who study for degrees who benefit from the presence of universities: it is everyone in society. As opposition MPs argued in the December 2010 House of Commons debate on tuition fees, it is not only when you send your children to school or drive on a motorway or go to the doctor or read a newspaper or make a phone call that you benefit from someone's university education – it's every time you turn on the tap.

We offer the following examples of the kinds of reorientation that will be required both within the academy and in the wider society. It is legitimate to criticize universities for a reluctance to communicate their ideas and knowledge to the general public. There are, indeed, some academics contemptuous of any such work and of their colleagues who do it, which is an attitude that should be rejected in all universities. It has to be recognized, however, that the Research Assessment Exercise (RAE), with its overwhelming emphasis on the value of research articles or monographs, has long made it impossible for academics to fulfil their 'research' contribution by writing popular works or even textbooks, so that those who wish to do them were obliged to do such work in addition to the requirements of the RAE. The 'Impact' agenda proposed for the Research Excellence Framework does little to address this problem, since it explicitly marginalizes academic or educational impact in favour of measurable economic impact. Since it is often more difficult and more time-consuming to synthesize a vast body of literature and to write it up in an accessible way than it is to carry out a piece of research, particularly if narrowly defined, then it is hardly surprising that many academics are reluctant to write for a general audience. There are other perverse effects.

Research that would make a good article gets written up as a book; short books are turned into long books in the hope that they will count as big books. But intellectually big books are discouraged, since they may well take longer than the assessment timeframe to produce. We are in danger of creating a world in which the big questions are never even asked, let alone answered.

It is also high time that journalists and others in public life stopped taking potshots at academics for the way that they write when they are writing for each other. All subjects have their own terminology, which can be used well to ensure conceptual clarity and precision, so that experts in the field know exactly what they are talking about, or can be used badly to mask poor thinking. Many of the debates in arts, humanities and social sciences turn upon terminology. It is an important element of the rigour of academic disciplines. To cite, out of context, a piece of academic jargon, written to be read by other academics, and to extrapolate from that the conclusion that academics are not interested in writing for a general audience, is wholly unfair. After all, you would surely not expect a brain surgeon to use the same language in a research paper as they would use when explaining to a patient what it means to have a brain tumour.

Academics share this responsibility, though. Academic life is tribal, and that has cost us dear. Even faced with the severity of the cuts, academics find it difficult to unite, even – perhaps especially – those from within the same subject. To take examples from the two fields we know best: cultural historians, theoretically inclined, often devote more energy to dismissing supposedly 'empiricist' military historians than they do to combating the debased idea of history as a mere adjunct to citizenship classes. Area studies people argue about exactly what is implied by the term instead of focusing on the fact that however it is defined it is being closed down across the country. Too often a legitimate concern about precision of language prevents academics from saying anything convincing to policy-makers. There are both good and bad reasons for academic tribalism: disciplines lose their edge if there is no vigilance over them; it is through comparative methodologies that rigorous approaches to evidence are preserved and developed; academics have now experienced over three decades of being compelled to compete for resources and all the incentives operate in favour of intensively working a small plot of earth rather than attempting to survey a field, let alone looking over the horizon to other lands.

Divisions occur not only by disciplinary fault-lines, but also between individuals who see themselves as pure researchers and others who communicate to a wider audience, often dismissed as 'popularizers'; between pre- and post- 1992 universities; between university managements and the majority of academic staff. Throughout the university sector, many people are manipulating the rules of the game to their own best advantage. 'Star' academics move from one fellowship to the next with the result that they hardly ever actually teach or even go to the institutions that pay their salaries and whose RAE ratings they are employed to improve. It is a zero-sum game, in which the person who did not win a fellowship will end up doing extra work to compensate for the absence of the lucky one who did. All of these everyday problems have to be understood at least partly as the consequences of the perverse incentives created by government policies, but there is no doubt that the collusion of academics has made it easier for policy-makers to divide and rule. And the tendency of at least some academics to affect lofty disdain for those beyond the ivory tower has also played into the hands of those who have a political interest in tapping the deep vein of anti-intellectualism that runs through Middle England. It would not have been so easy for Mrs Thatcher to score a cheap point by attacking the 'cloister and the common room' for denigrating the creators of wealth in Britain had there not been an element of truth in what she said. It would be welcome to see more academics doing more to challenge such attitudes.

Under the new social contract for universities there will still be a role for the state to play in ensuring accountability; the challenge will be to design ways of stimulating what Onora O'Neill (2002) has called 'intelligent accountability'. She means conditions in which there are obligations to tell the truth; in which people think less about their rights (what they should get) and more about their responsibilities (what they should do); in which agency means not just choosing one constrained option over another, but, rather, being a position to have a meaningful say about the values and practices that shape their environment. Conditions, in short, in which perverse incentives, such as those created by the RAE, are avoided.[5] And universities need to grasp the nettle of what to do about people who are not very good at their jobs, not by multiplying the performance indicators that all too often allow the mediocre to tick enough boxes to stay in post, but by establishing rigorous reviews, perhaps at five-yearly intervals, throughout an academic career.

Conclusion

If we are to break out of the inspection-house and reclaim the university as a place in which academics, students and other interested parties can devote themselves to learning, critical reflection and debate, there needs to be a widespread recognition across society of the value of the academic freedom that is about to be destroyed. It is in the capacity of intellectuals to interpret and make sense of the world, and to question received truths, that their true value lies. The English language lacks a generic noun for intellectual work, or the systematic development of knowledge and understanding, which is captured so well in the German term *Wissenschaft*. 'Science' served the purpose until the 1830s, but then experimentalists coined the term 'scientist' and a general term became one for denoting the natural sciences. Another German term conveys what intellectuals do: *Sinnstiftung*. Tellingly untranslatable it means interpreting and making sense of the world.

The conditions of the twenty-first century create important opportunities for universities: to focus on thinking dispassionately, critically and rigorously, untrammelled by the illusions of universal reason and national culture; to ask big questions and to help answer them by overcoming artificial divides, such as those between the humanities and the sciences or between specialists and generalists; to democratize, both in terms of participation and in terms of institutional openness; and to open up new channels for two-way communication with society. With a new contract between the universities and the state, based on responsibility, trust and intelligent accountability, the British higher education sector could become genuinely open, democratic and international – in short, fit for the demands of the twenty-first century. Can Britain really afford not to take these opportunities?

4

Science as a Public Good

Philip Moriarty

A change in culture

I have a confession to make. It's a difficult admission in the current
funding climate for academics in the UK, but here it is: I am a scientist.
Not an engineer. Not a technologist. And certainly not an entrepreneur. I
pursue basic research into fundamental questions about the properties of
matter on a variety of different length scales (ranging, in my case, from
sub-atomic to sub-millimetre dimensions), in common with a very large
number of my colleagues working in the physical and life sciences in
British universities. Whether or not this research can be translated into a
marketable product, exploited as profitable intellectual property (IP), or
applied in technology is not what motivates me. My motivation, again
in common with the majority of academic scientists in the UK,[1] lies in
improving our understanding of nature, generating (not protecting) new
knowledge, and disseminating my findings to other scientists, students
and society at large.

Despite their regular claims to the contrary (which I dissect below),
this 'traditional' view of the societal value of scientific research is
now anathema both to Research Councils UK (RCUK), the umbrella
organization for the seven research councils which fund the bulk of
academic research in the UK, and to the Higher Education Funding
Council for England (HEFCE). Since 2007 there has been a series of
changes to RCUK funding strategies with the primary aim of inculcating
a 'culture change' in academic science, so as to 'shorten the innovation
chain' (Corbyn 2009). Government initiatives to make academia more
'business-facing' have, of course, a rather longer history, as also outlined
below but described at length elsewhere (for example, Finlayson and

Hayward 2010; Langley and Parkinson 2009). In parallel with the changes to RCUK policy, HEFCE has introduced an analysis and ranking of socioeconomic 'impact' into its Research Excellence Framework – the primary vehicle for the assessment of academic research in UK universities and the determinant of the allocation of the so-called quality-related (QR) component of the HEFCE budget to UK universities.

In this chapter I will critique RCUK's and HEFCE's strategies to enhance the socioeconomic impact of scientific research (the so-called impact agenda) by their 'incentivization' of UK academics to target problems of direct short-term socioeconomic interest. Not only do the research/funding council strategies run counter to the ethos of publicly funded academic science, and significantly compromise the societal value (and trustworthiness) of university research, but they are, perhaps counter-intuitively, of *economically* questionable value.

The issues I raise are, of course, far from new; the arguments regarding the cultural, economic and societal value of *disinterested*, curiosity-driven research have been convincingly made for many decades by commentators and researchers in a broad variety of fields. My aim, however, is to place these arguments in the context of the current funding climate for academic scientists in the UK and to describe how changes to the policies and strategies of the UK funding bodies over the last five years will have dramatic and irrevocable effects on the ethos, trustworthiness, creativity and socioeconomic impact of university science.

Merton (1942) and Ziman (2000), in particular, have highlighted the central importance of the disinterestedness of scientists in attacking a research problem. While many might argue, with strong justification, that the traditional picture of objective, entirely rational scientists seeking the truth is far from an accurate portrayal of scientific activity (Ziman himself frequently disparages this as 'the Legend', for example), disinterestedness is nonetheless at the very heart of the scientific method. It is something that all scientists must strive to achieve if their work is to be trustworthy and of value to not only their peers but to science and society in general. As Ziman put it, 'Disinterested science is essentially a moral enterprise sustained by a tacit ethos of mutual trust. This ethos is being fatally undermined by enforced cohabitation with instrumental research' (2002: 399). As I will show in the following sections, not only are RCUK and HEFCE not concerned about the erosion of disinterested science in UK universities, they are actively driving its demise.

Of course, one can argue that the socioeconomic and sociopolitical 'landscape' in twenty-first century British society differs distinctly from that in decades gone by and that funding strategies that were workable in the 1970s, for example, may be rather less viable in 2011. But this rather misses the key point: the qualities and attributes of good science from the 1970s – or any other decade for that matter – are precisely the same as those in the twenty-first century[2]. The ultimate goal of the RCUK/HEFCE impact agenda is not to improve the quality of UK science (which, by a variety of metrics, is already at the very least internationally competitive and, in a range of fields, of world-leading standing). Rather, it is to drive universities to become not only business-facing but *business-led*, involving an evolution of academic science from a public to a private good, and a concomitant focus on utilitarian, near-market and applied research. Remarkably, and rather cannily on the part of the funding bodies, this highly damaging corruption of the ethos of the university is 'sold' as being entirely in the public interest.

Eroding the Mertonian norms

In a highly influential paper, Robert K. Merton laid down the attributes of what he termed the normative structure of science (Merton 1942). Merton initially put forward four sets of what he called institutional imperatives comprising the scientific ethos, namely universalism, commun(al)ism, disinterestedness and scepticism.[3] It is worth quoting from Merton at length because it is remarkable just how valuable his insights remain seventy years after their publication. On the communism norm he wrote:

> Communism, in the nontechnical and extended sense of common ownership of goods, is [an] integral element of the scientific ethos. The substantive findings of science are a product of social collaboration and are assigned to the community. They constitute a common heritage in which the equity of the individual producer is severely limited. An eponymous law or theory does not enter into the exclusive possession of the discovered and his heirs, nor do the mores bestow upon them special rights of use and disposition. (1942: 270)

Compare Merton's eloquent espousal of the common ownership of scientific ideas and discoveries with a number of statements in the RCUK response to the Lambert Review of business-university collaboration:

[The Natural Environment Research Council]'s interest in business-university collaboration is to support the transfer of knowledge from producers (NERC funded scientists) to business users ... NERC places a high priority on supporting links between NERC funded researchers and the business community, and business views are considered at all levels of decision making. (RCUK 2003: 19)

[A] focus of the [Particle Physics and Astronomy Research Council] PPARC[4] is encouraging an entrepreneurial culture, particularly at the early stages of a research career ... to help commercialise ideas originating from PPARC funding – usually in the form of start-up companies. We would be happy to work with senior management and technology transfer offices in universities to help change the culture towards encouraging business links and entrepreneurship in physics departments. (RCUK 2003: 21–2)

[The Biotechnology and Biological Sciences Research Council] BBSRC takes the view that commercial activity is best performed by the research generator and therefore delegates responsibility for the identification, management and exploitation of IP arising from research supported by Council to the university or institute undertaking that research. (RCUK 2003: 6)

The contrast between the Mertonian norm of communalism and the research councils' drive to embed an entrepreneurial culture in academic science could not be more stark. This focus on commercialization, IP-derived income streams and entrepreneurship has developed and strengthened considerably since the Lambert Review in 2003. Following hot on the heels of Lambert's report came the publication of the Warry (2006), Leitch (Leitch 2006) and Sainsbury (2007) reviews. In each case, the emphasis was on developing the 'business-facing' character of British universities via the protection, rather than free dissemination, of scientific knowledge so that it could be commercially exploited as intellectual property.

What is particularly disturbing about RCUK's strong commitment to the development of an entrepreneurial academic culture is that the research councils were perfectly happy to abrogate all responsibility for the management and exploitation of IP to the universities and institutions/

companies involved in the research, despite that intellectual property having been generated from public funds disbursed by the councils. (See, for example, the final quote from the RCUK response to the Leitch review above.) It is only very recently that RCUK has attempted to address this issue by adding a statement to its expectations regarding the exploitation of intellectual property: 'The Research Councils may, in individual cases, reserve the right to retain ownership of intellectual property and to arrange for it to be exploited for the national benefit in other ways' (RCUK 2011). While including this proviso is laudable, a cynic might ask quite how often RCUK will 'retain ownership' of IP for the public good. In any case, Langley and Parkinson (Langley and Parkinson 2009) have provided compelling evidence that RCUK-funded research is increasingly driven by narrow commercial imperatives rather than being motivated by either scientific curiosity or the wider public benefit. In fact, public benefit is made equivalent to the contribution to economic growth organized in terms of private interest.

Although a discussion of RCUK and HEFCE funding policy in the context of all five Mertonian norms would be instructive, I would like to focus here instead on just one other norm, *disinterestedness*, given its central importance in the scientific method. It is the erosion of disinterested research – implicitly coupled, of course, with the demise of the norm of communalism – that is arguably most damaging to publicly funded science in the UK.

A key aspect of the disinterestedness norm is perhaps best summed up by the pithy proclamation attributed to Einstein: 'If we knew what we were doing, it wouldn't be called research, would it?' Scientists involved in fundamental research are traditionally driven by curiosity – they carry out their work not to 'engage with users' nor to 'generate impact' but to address a question, or series of questions, about how nature behaves. If, in attempting to answer that question, they discover serendipitously a more interesting avenue of research then they should be free to 'follow their nose' and explore because no one knows where that particular line of enquiry might lead. Their research may, of course, ultimately have quite remarkable economic and societal spin-offs but that is not the original motivation for carrying out the work.

Basic scientific research – also variously labelled fundamental, or blue skies, or curiosity-driven science – is a process of exploration and discovery with, in the best cases, a strong dose of creativity and imagination added to the mix. The distinction between applied and fundamental research is a vexed issue, with scientists themselves generally struggling to delineate the two activities (Calvert 2006), but it is certainly possible to distinguish between the extremes on the applied-fundamental continuum, i.e. between near-term activities targeted at addressing market-led technology development (that is, research which is closer to the 'D' component of 'R&D') and exploratory, disinterested science which is focused on answering fundamental questions about nature with little or no concern for potential applicability. The difficulty with attempting to attach labels such as basic/blueskies applied/curiosity-driven to these distinct types of science is that different sectors can have conflicting interpretations of the labels. For example, the 2009 'Global R&D Funding Forecast' by Battelle makes the important point that:

> The term 'basic research' as interpreted and applied by industry is not the same as that employed by other sectors. In general, the term as applied in an industrial context is perhaps better defined as 'directed basic research', i.e. generally directed toward activities in support of the lines of business,[5] rather than pure research that's directed toward establishing a baseline of knowledge. (2009: 11)

Charting the boundaries between 'pure' and 'applied' science is thus fraught with difficulties.[6] For example, the oft-derided linear model is perhaps not quite as flawed a description of the 'innovation eco-system' – or, at least, certain key aspects of that system – as is traditionally thought (Balconi, Brusoni and Orsenigo 2010). Nonetheless, the Mertonian norms – particularly those of communalism and disinterestedness – remain as a set of guiding principles which can be used to broadly distinguish traditional academic science from the commercialized, entrepreneurial and near-market scientific R&D that is increasingly promoted (either directly or indirectly) by the UK research and funding councils. But to what extent do the Mertonian norms stand up to scrutiny in the twenty-first century? Are they seen by working scientists simply as a bygone relic of a largely apocryphal 'golden' age or are they viewed as an integral 'value set' for modern science? If the latter holds true, then there exists a striking and damaging conflict between the research councils' oft-stated aim to establish an entrepreneurial culture and the motivations of academic scientists.

Mertonian myths?

Anderson *et al.* (2010) have published the results of focus group interviews and national survey studies that have sought to elucidate the extent to which US scientists subscribe to the Mertonian norms. Theirs is an important and timely paper which, despite highlighting the limitations associated with any attempt to provide a definitive 'normative structure' for science (whether complemented by counter-norms or not), shows that subscription to the Mertonian norms amongst US scientists is very high (ranging from 73 per cent to 91 per cent of the scientists involved in their study). As Anderson *et al.* put it, 'The Mertonian norms, as principles representative of the normative system of science, have been challenged, attacked, dismissed, contested, inconsistently referenced, and, in short, battered and bruised by controversy and careless application. They nonetheless have endured for over 65 years as part of the communal property of science' (2010: 391).

Anderson *et al.* provide a helpful summary of the more high profile critiques to which they allude in the quote above, highlighting Mulkay's criticisms (Mulkay 1976) in particular. Mulkay argued that Merton's norms represent nothing more than the expectations of 'outsiders', i.e. they act simply to enforce a particular 'external' stereotype which does not really represent the scientific process – rather than providing an accurate picture of the social interactions and expectations underpinning the day-to-day activities of scientists. A significant number of sociologists have raised similar criticisms, to the extent that Hess, for example, has argued that 'For decades the consensus among social scientists has been that, as descriptions of the norms that actually guide scientists' action, Merton's norms do not exist in any pervasive form' (1997: 57). And yet Anderson *et al.* find that the Mertonian norms 'resonate' strongly with a large majority of the US scientists they surveyed (without, of course, those norms being explicitly 'taught' in the majority of cases). This appears at first glance to be somewhat paradoxical.

The reconciliation of the traditional sociological view of the Mertonian norms with the results of Anderson *et al.*'s study lies in the idealized nature of the CUDOS principles. As Anderson and her co-authors note, Hess qualifies the statement quoted above with the important observation that, 'It is possible to salvage Merton's delineation of the norms of science, but only as a prescription of how scientists should behave ideally' (1997: 57). Kellog makes much the same point but rather more expansively:

> Yet though Merton's particular form of analysis may seem outdated from one perspective, the norms he named in 1942 have persisted impressively in public understanding. We still tend to assume that science follows the Mertonian framework – or would, if social factors did not keep getting in the way. Of course claims should be evaluated on their merit, not on who made them; of course scientific knowledge should be open to inspection and evaluation; of course personal interests should be subordinated to the scientific enterprise; of course the institutions of science should pursue rigorous testing of hypotheses. Such views are hardly controversial; they represent the conventional wisdom about what we think, or what we hope, science to be. (The status of such views as conventional wisdom helps explain the widespread resistance among scientists to strong claims by the sociology of science, which are taken as attacking the realization, if not the ambition, of scientific practice.) (2006: 6)

Given Kellog's assertion that the Mertonian norms have 'persisted impressively' in the public perception of science, it is perhaps hardly surprising that Anderson *et al.* find that the majority of scientists strongly subscribe to them. While it may be difficult, in the face of a broad array of internal and external sociological factors, for scientists always to uphold the Mertonian ideals, one might at least hope that public funding agencies would aim to establish an academic environment that protects, rather than erodes, Merton's norms.[7] This, however, is certainly not the case. Perhaps the most dispiriting aspect of the RCUK/HEFCE impact agenda is that, under the guise of greater public accountability, it fosters a culture in UK academic science that is at odds, to a greater or lesser extent, with each of the values represented by the CUDOS acronym.

CUDOS vs PLACE, Mode 2 vs Mode 1, 'Post-academia' vs Academia?

In *Real Science: What it is, and What it Means* (2000), John Ziman compares the norms of industrial science with those of academic science, neatly encapsulating the inherent friction between the two cultures in the 'PLACE' acronym (to contrast with Merton's 'CUDOS'). Industrial science is proprietary (as opposed to communalist); local (not universal); authoritarian (vs disinterested); commissioned (as opposed to original);

and expert (rather than sceptical).[8] The contrast with academic science is striking; attempting to embed the PLACE norms within the Mertonian scientific worldview necessitates a convergence of diametrically opposed cultures and working practices. While one can, of course, convincingly argue that the industrial/academic science division is far from as clear-cut as the PLACE/CUDOS comparison would suggest, merging the two modes of research nonetheless requires a jarring clash of cultures.

Ziman referred to the convergence of industrial and academic science as *post-academic*. Others have used the term 'Mode 2' research (Gibbons *et al.* 1994), where 'Mode 1' is in essence what is described as academic or 'Mertonian' science. There are subtle, and not-so-subtle, differences between Ziman's concept of post-academia and Mode 2 research and it is worth spending a moment to disentangle the two. Helga Nowotny, currently President of the European Research Council and one of the authors of the seminal paper which introduced the 'Mode 2' concept, has eloquently described the differences between post-academic and Mode-2 research (Nowotny 2006). The key distinction is that Ziman saw the evolution of post-academic science as representing the death of the Mertonian norms, where instead of disinterested publicly funded scientists seeking after 'the truth' (however 'the truth' might be defined), in post-academia 'socio-economic power is the final authority' (Ziman 2000; 174), with scientific creativity and exploration eventually succumbing to external governmental and/or industrial pressures for near-term or near-market applicability.

Nowotny, while still a staunch and passionate advocate of blue-skies research, is rather more optimistic and, along with her colleagues, argues that curiosity-driven science is sufficiently robust to endure socioeconomic, governmental and industrial pressures. I, unfortunately, do not share Nowotny's optimism. Scientific curiosity, disinterestedness and creativity are all adversely affected by the UK research and funding councils' impact agenda, either directly via grant funding decisions or indirectly via universities' encouragement of academics to skew their research towards work which aligns more readily with RCUK/HEFCE strategic priorities and/or demonstrates a short-term impact that can be readily quantified. The indirect incentivization pathway is crucial: university management is entirely complicit in the erosion of the ethos of academic science.

The impact agenda: facilitating the expansion of post-academic science in the UK

In summary, the Mertonian norms are being systematically eroded in British academia via the RCUK/HEFCE 'impact agenda' (and associated policies) and the compliance of university management, facilitating a rapid acceleration in the development of a post-academic/Mode 2 culture. The Engineering and Physical Sciences Research Council (EPSRC) is an especially interesting case in this regard because, in addition to the requirement for grant applicants to describe the 'pathways to impact' of their research (as also expected by all other research councils), EPSRC explicitly stated as part of its 2011–2014 Delivery Plan that it will move from being a funder to a sponsor of research, 'where [its] investments act as a national resource focussed on outcomes for the UK good' (EPSRC 2011: 6). EPSRC's evolution from funder to sponsor is an archetypal example of the inculcation of a post-academic culture in university science and thus warrants careful study.[9] In order to understand the impetus for the funder-to-sponsor transition, it will be helpful to first briefly outline the history of EPSRC's (and RCUK's) strategy to embed an assessment of potential (socio)economic impact in the peer review process – the so-called 'impact agenda'. The impact agenda and EPSRC's adoption of the role of research sponsor are complementary aspects of the drive to ensure greater near-term 'responsiveness' of academic research to socioeconomic pressures. Ziman's writings on the evolution of post-academic science, and his pessimism with regard to the extinction of academic science, can be seen as remarkably prescient in the context of the impact agenda.

The recent history of the UK government's efforts to encourage industrial engagement with academic science is long and tortuously involved. Langley and Parkinson (2009) provide a helpful timeline of major milestones in the commercialization of UK universities, spanning the Faraday Partnerships scheme set up by the Department of Trade and Industry in 1991; the publication of Waldegrave's *Realising our Potential* White Paper in 1993; the Roberts, Lambert, Warry, Leitch, and Sainsbury reports from 2002 to 2007 respectively; through to the creation of the Department of Business, Innovation and Skills in 2009 under the New Labour government. I will focus entirely on events since the publication of the Warry Report in 2006 which set in motion the research councils' drive to accelerate the establishment of a 'post-academic' or 'Mode 2' culture via the impact agenda (Warry Report 2006).

The Warry Report was very clear in its ambitions regarding culture change in British academia (echoing Waldegrave's aspiration to 'to achieve a key cultural change... between the scientific community, industry, and government departments' (1993: 5). Entitled *Increasing the Economic Impact of the Research Councils*, the key recommendations of the report were as follows:

> Chairs of Research Councils should ensure that economic impact is given a high profile in Council strategy ... One of the Research Council chief executives should be nominated by RCUK to champion the work on economic impact across all Councils. (Warry Report 2006: 3) [This led to the creation of the 'RCUK Impact Champion' post.]

> The Research Councils should influence the behaviour of universities, research institutes and Funding Councils in ways that will increase the economic impact of Research Council funding. (Warry Report 2006: 3)

> RCUK should engage Government, business and the public services in a wide-ranging dialogue to develop overarching, economically relevant research missions. These missions should address major strategic challenges for the UK ... [and] be in areas where the UK wishes to become a world leader (e.g. Energy, Creative Industries and eScience). (Warry Report 2006: 4)

> Research Councils [should] allocate a substantial part of their funding to programmes relevant to their user communities. These programmes should engage economic stakeholders; form part of each Research Council's overall strategic plan; give greater prominence to follow-on funding to develop promising research results to a stage where they attract external investment. (Warry Report 2006: 4-5)

On the matter of peer review, Warry made the following proposals. Note the incorporation of a strong element of *user* review (which, as Finlayson and Hayward [2009] pointedly note, is not the same thing at all as *peer* review) and the remarkably naive suggestion that scientists and other academics can be trained to accurately assess – indeed, 'score' (i.e. rank) – the economic impact of grant proposals.

Research Councils should ensure that:

- Peer review panels contain members expert in identifying work of potential economic importance;

- Reviewers' training includes the importance of economic relevance to the overall Council mission;

- Guidelines for reviewers are clear on how they should score the economic impact of bids and how this score is related to the other measures by which bids are assessed. (Warry Report 2006: 5)

Shortly following the publication of the Warry Report, RCUK carried out a consultation on the efficiency and effectiveness of peer review (RCUK 2006). On the matter of the Warry Report's recommendations on peer review of economic impact, RCUK asked the following questions and invited universities, learned societies, professional bodies, research institutes and so on to respond: 'Without compromising research quality, how could Research Councils develop the peer review process to ensure that potential economic impact is effectively reflected within proposal assessment? How can Research Councils ensure that reviewers have the skills, experience and information necessary to assess effectively potential economic impact?' (2006: 4)

The response to the consultation on the issue of the inclusion of economic impact criteria in peer review was overwhelmingly negative (RCUK 2007).[10] For example, the University of Cambridge responded as follows: 'We find this part of the consultation somewhat baffling. ... To assess potential impact of a research proposal, beyond potential application (as is already done), before the research is undertaken, at the granularity of an individual proposal, is patently silly.' North of the border, the University of Glasgow was similarly baffled:

We believe the recommendations of the Warry report related to the peer review process to be worryingly naïve. The connection between a specific research project and economic impact is difficult if not impossible to evaluate. Economic impact itself is not a well-defined concept supported by a body of theory enabling the calculation of an economic impact factor. The economic impact of a research project may not be made for decades after the research has been completed, and often not in the research field itself.

The University of Nottingham was, if anything, even more perplexed than both Cambridge and Glasgow: 'This option appears to fly in the face of the purpose of "research" within universities … could stifle highly imaginative, original and creative work, or lead to dubious, often irrefutable, claims in many areas of science – especially fundamental/"blue skies" research.'

But this was a consultation in the best New Labour sense of the term. Thus, the concerns voiced by the majority of the respondents regarding inclusion of economic impact criteria in peer review were effectively ignored by RCUK. EPSRC introduced an assessment of economic impact[11] into the peer review process in April 2009 (and was met with silence by those very many universities who had strongly criticized the inclusion of economic impact criteria as 'patently silly' and 'worryingly naive'). From that date onwards all grant applicants have been required to submit a two-page 'impact statement' outlining how their research has the potential to 'foster global economic performance, and specifically the economic competitiveness of the United Kingdom', 'increase the effectiveness of public services and policy', and/or 'enhance quality of life, health, and creative output' (RCUK 2009). Moreover, applicants are expected to define 'realistic timescales for the benefits to be realized' (RCUK 2009). Following EPSRC's introduction of the impact statement requirement, the other research councils followed suit.

The Mertonian norms are clearly heavily compromised by the requirement that scientists lay out the socioeconomic impact of their research in advance (with their proposals subsequently judged and ranked on the basis of alignment with those short-term/near-market objectives). The extent to which the disinterestedness norm has been eroded is perhaps best illustrated by RCUK's 'Top ten tips for completing the "pathways to impact" statement' (RCUK 2010). Tip number one on this list is 'Draft the Impact Summary very early in your preparation, so that it informs the design of your research.' Similarly, tip five tells us that, 'Most proposals aim to engage with beneficiaries and end users. Where possible, and for impact activities to be more effective, end users should be involved from the outset of the research design process to maximise the potential up-take and application of the research.' In other words, define the outcomes, users and beneficiaries of your work and design the research project accordingly. This is not how scientific research proceeds; it is a prescription more in line with the 'D' component of a near-market R&D programme (and thus entirely consistent with RCUK's stated aim to shorten the innovation chain).

In parallel with RCUK's 'Pathways to Impact' initiative, HEFCE modified its Research Assessment Exercise (RAE) to incorporate 'impact' as a criterion with a weighting of 20 per cent (the RAE was renamed the Research Excellence Framework, REF, in 2007). Echoing the research councils' response to the negative feedback it received on the question of introducing economic impact criteria in peer review, HEFCE dismissed a petition, organized by the University and College Union and signed by 17,500 academics (including six Nobel laureates), which called for the withdrawal of the inclusion of a consideration of impact in the REF. The petition argued that, 'The REF proposals are founded on a lack of understanding of how knowledge advances. It is often difficult to predict which research will create the greatest practical impact. History shows us that in many instances it is curiosity-driven research that has led to major scientific and cultural advances' (University and College Union 2009).

For the public good?

RCUK and HEFCE repeatedly make the argument that the impact agenda is simply a mechanism to enhance public accountability and to improve the return on taxpayers' investment in research. University researchers who oppose the impact agenda are cast by HEFCE/RCUK as reactionary ivory tower academics who are unwilling to accept that academic research must contribute to the public good – a deeply frustrating straw-man argument. I have argued that by compromising the Mertonian norms to the extent required by the impact agenda, the UK research and funding councils do not enhance the public good aspects of academic science. Instead, they are driving publicly funded university research ever-closer to the PLACE norms of industrial science. Far from improving accountability and transparency, this will embed a culture of intellectual property protection and commercial exploitation entirely at odds with the ethos of academia and, ultimately, compromising public trust in science (something increasingly significant in the light of risks of global warming and food sustainability).

But does a focus on protecting knowledge and intellectual property generated from publicly funded science, with all the associated compromises regarding the openness, reliability and trustworthiness of academic research, actually pay off in terms of economic benefit? Richard

R. Nelson, in a highly cited paper, considered the relationship between the market economy and the publicly supported 'scientific commons', highlighting that, 'the perception of how the modern science system actually works has eroded the notion that it is important to keep science open' (2004: 457). This is 'a serious mistake' and Nelson – a serious and sober commentator hardly given to fits of hyperbole – wants to 'call the alarm'. Citing a number of classics in science funding policy – including Vannevar Bush's *Science the Endless Frontier* (1945) and Polanyi's 'The republic of science' (1967) – Nelson eloquently lays out the intrinsic tension that exists between the norms of the publicly funded science base and, as he puts it, the 'capitalist engine' of scientific advancement. While admitting that there are deficiencies in the Mertonian view of science, Nelson strongly argued that the communal (or 'communitarian') aspects of science are, as economists have long argued, key to extracting the greatest level of public value from university research. Nelson makes a very strong statement on the importance of maintaining science in the public domain: 'To privatize basic knowledge is a danger both for the advance of science, and for the advance of technology' (2004: 456).

Yet, as detailed throughout this chapter, the Research Councils UK argue that what is required of academic science is a culture change such that university researchers become more entrepreneurial and, thus, focus on the wealth-creating/spin-off/IP potential of their research. In the research councils' view this somehow has the potential simultaneously to shorten the innovation chain and to ensure the integrity of curiosity-driven research. As Nelson and many others have pointed out, however, the two approaches to academic science – entrepreneurial/market-driven R&D vs open science carried out in the spirit of the Mertonian norms – are diametrically opposed and 'enforced co-habitation', to use Ziman's description, dramatically undermines curiosity-driven research. What is perhaps less intuitive is that a focus on near-market deliverables and the privatization of the results of scientific research has the potential to be *economically* damaging, i.e. to reduce, rather than enhance, return on government investment in research. Due to the introduction, over thirty years ago, of legislation specifically targeted at enhancing the commercial uptake of academic research, i.e. the Bayh–Dole Act of 1980, US academia represents an important model system in which to analyse the merits and demerits of attempts to embed an entrepreneurial culture in academia.

US Congress passed the Bayh–Dole Act to address what was perceived to be a major problem with the commercialization of (federally funded) academic research, namely state ownership of intellectual property rights. Bayh–Dole allowed universities, and federally contracted research carried out by other types of institution, to patent inventions arising from publicly funded research. While Bayh–Dole was heralded in some quarters as a boon to the US economy and society in general, there has been a steadily increasing number of papers that have questioned whether the university invention ownership model for which the Act legislates has actually driven greater economic efficiency or has improved the public value of discoveries and inventions arising from academic science and engineering. Nelson was far from an enthusiastic fan of Bayh–Dole, arguing that, 'long prior to Bayh–Dole, the American university research system had a well known record of strong performance in doing research that contributed to technical progress and industrial development, and strong efforts in technology transfer. The latter almost always was accomplished without the university claiming any intellectual property rights' (2001: 16). Nelson made strong economic arguments that intellectual property rights should not be associated with fundamental discoveries, even calling for patent law to be rewritten so as to prohibit universities from patenting the results of basic research. In a remarkably strongly worded editorial in 2004, the *Lancet* echoed Nelson's concerns, stating that 'academics have a choice – to develop their entrepreneurial skills or to maintain a commitment to public-interest science – and we do not accept that the two options are mutually compatible' (James *et al*, 2004).

Nelson's strong criticism of Bayh–Dole was followed by a considerable number of similarly critical papers and books (including Washburn 2005 and Greenberg 2007). Fabrizio (2007) puts forward strong evidence that a focus on university patenting slows, rather than accelerates, knowledge transfer to industry. Kenney and Patton (2009) identify a series of deficiencies in the Bayh–Dole model and put forward two possible solutions – vesting ownership of any invention with the inventor or, more radically, to place information regarding all publicly funded inventions and discoveries in the public domain. They are stinging in their criticism of those policy-makers who attempt to mimic the US university invention/patent ownership model and disagree strongly with the Organisation for Economic Co-operation and Development (OECD)'s *Turning Science into Business: Patenting and Licensing at Public Research Organisations* report (2003), which claims that there is a pressing need to generate support for university patenting and related activities. A similar 'urgency' regarding patent and spin-off generation from academic research is found in almost every European Commission document focused on the European Research Area in the context of the multibillion euro Framework Programmes. It is therefore perhaps not too surprising to note that there is a strong focus on patent and spin-off generation in the physics case study examples selected from the Research Excellent Framework Impact pilot study (HEFCE 2010).

Ironically, the key motivation for the introduction of the impact agenda is that university scientists are expected to 'pick up the slack' for deficiencies elsewhere in the UK innovation system. But innovation, as typically understood by the government and industry, cannot be driven by 'Mertonian' science (whose orientation is much too long term). Scientific research in academia is of course a key source of innovation but currently not on timescales that are sufficiently customer- or 'stakeholder'-focused for industry and government. It is the short-term incremental innovation identified by Kline and Rosenberg (1986) that private industry (and therefore government) is so keen to foster in universities. The fine words of David Willetts, UK Minister for Universities and Science, regarding the fundamental role of academic research in improving the 'absorptive capacity' of society (quoted in Jump 2010) have been quickly forgotten in the drive to make university science more 'business facing'.

While it is perhaps not so surprising that politicians do not appreciate the benefits of university science – and, indeed, higher education in general – as anything other than a key contributor to the 'knowledge-based economy'– what is perhaps most dispiriting about the impact agenda is the extent to which the research councils and, most worryingly of all, universities themselves have abandoned any commitment to truly disinterested, curiosity-driven research 'whose applications may take time to emerge, if [they do] at all' (to quote David Willetts again). Before drawing up yet another strategy document aiming to 'incentivize' academics to maximize the value of the intellectual property they 'generate' and/or deliver maximum impact from their research, each vice-chancellor and pro-vice chancellor in the UK should be obligated to read and reflect on Boulton and Lucas's words on the societal role of the university:

> Universities are not just supermarkets for a variety of public and private goods that are currently in demand, and whose value is defined by their

perceived aggregate financial value. We assert that they have a deeper, fundamental role that permits them to adapt and respond to the changing values and needs of successive generations, and from which the outputs cherished by governments are but secondary derivatives. To define the university enterprise by these specific outputs, and to fund it only through metrics that measure them, is to misunderstand the nature of the enterprise and its potential to deliver social benefit. (2008: 17)

5

The Politics of
Publicly-funded Social Research[1]

Desmond King

The current economic crisis enveloping the advanced democratic world since 2007 has not only led to the election of a new public finances austerity-committed administration in the UK, formed of a Conservative-Liberal coalition, but has sparked enormous changes in the world of university funding and public research support. This latter issue extends across all areas of academic enquiry – medicine, humanities, natural sciences and social sciences. In each area vigorous campaigns led by university-based scientists have warned about the dangers of under-investment, particularly in pure research. Applied research has fared better in the recent years but researchers continually underline the importance of doing pure research for the country's long-term development of knowledge. The shift to greater funding for applied research correlates to the more general move to fee-based courses and user responsiveness in the UK university sector.

As such this development marks a major change in public expectations about universities in the British polity and political economy. The expansion of public funding for social research commenced in the post-war social democratic consensus about state planning and the need for accurate empirical data to guide social programmes aimed at amelioration and social mobility. This consensual view faced its first major challenge and reform under the shift to neo-liberalism that developed after the economic and social crises of the 1970s, and was expressed in public policy enacted under the Conservative government led by Mrs Thatcher. This second stage included a rigorous review of the social science research agency, which induced funding instability and political uncertainty for the Social Science Research Council (SSRC), renamed the Economic and Social Research Council (ESRC) in 1983, but accepted the value and appropriateness of the public funding of a plurality of social and economic research, some of the findings of which might be politically unpalatable for the prevailing government. A continuity of language between the first and second eras permitted the principle of critical research findings. However, since 2010 a third phase in the state funding of social research has unfolded in which it is increasingly linked to measurements of impact, that is, the impact that the findings of publicly funded research has on policy decisions – in the language of the ESRC, its interest in research aimed at 'influencing behaviour and informing intervention'. This third phase retains some continuity of language with the previous eras in terms of acceptance of the need for publicly funded social research. But its location in an era of high-austerity public finances and prioritization of impact in the parallel research assessment process (the Research Excellence Framework 2014 exercise) mean that, beneath outward signs of continuity of assumptions and language, there may be considerable change in the content and scope of how publicly funded research is understood. The key issue – which will only be addressed over the next few years – is whether the production of knowledge critical of prevailing ideas and policy assumptions continues. As the current economic crisis demonstrates, fostering critical views of our understanding of how basic economic, social and political processes operate is a key task of social researchers and a fundamental obligation of the public university.

Towards public funding of social research

Since the public funding of research began in the twentieth century and especially as it expanded massively from the 1940s, a single contentious question about this investment developed and recurred: should public funding of research require measurable results in applied outputs or should it finance basic science or basic research? In practice it does both. But the perceived conflict between the two activities has been a dominant theme particularly in the politics of social research (though it features, too, in the world of natural science funding). Several sub-themes have flowed from this core issue. First, what methodology is most suitable to social research? Should it be a positivist framework broadly imitative of the natural sciences or a methodology distinct to the specific issues involved in measuring the social world? And how tied should publicly funded social research be to research themes or intellectual questions formulated by governments through research councils. In the UK these issues have been there since the SSRC/ESRC was founded in 1965. Moments of salience include the early 1980s when Prime Minister Margaret Thatcher's Education Secretary, Sir Keith Joseph, ordered an investigation into the research council, certain that it funded inappropriate or trivial research questions. The investigation, in fact, vindicated the research council (though compelling a change of name) and since then its existence has not been in doubt (Rothschild Report 1982).

However, the purpose of the ESRC has been subject to wide discussion. At the founding of the SSRC, there was considerable discussion of how the new body should fund research activity in respect to content (applied or basic research) and to the degree of guidance (should the council structure grants with its own themes or solicit individual applications?). What has changed now is the extent to which the ESRC's funding shapes the content of research activity in social science. For critics, the council's agenda of strategic or thematic priorities runs the danger of squeezing other lines of research activity because it reduces the funds available to them.

Pursuing an increasingly utilitarian conception of research and, in particular, articulating broad research themes, partly in tandem with government priorities, the ESRC's role as the agent of research funding is one balanced on a tightrope. I will suggest in this chapter that while the ESRC has mostly avoided falling into an excessively pro-government stance in supporting research funding, its most recent statement of principles brings it perilously close. The agenda has firmly shifted toward funding and producing government-friendly research findings about what policies work or how policy can influence individual or household behaviour. Gone is any debate about the appropriateness of engaging in particular policy.

The most recent list of strategic priorities issued by the ESRC emphasizes the themes of (a) economic performance and sustainable growth, (b) influencing behaviour and informing interventions, and (c) a vibrant and fair society (ESRC 2010). However, the council underlines on its website that these three priorities are 'not a steer to how research grants will be made'.[2] Nonetheless the ESRC wants to be relevant to government as its discussion of these three priorities reveals. Research grants will continue to be made on the basis of peer review, but the topics deemed appropriate to study are shaped by the priorities. With universities keen to increase research-funding success, their own research priorities are increasingly adjusted to those of the research councils with a further narrowing of perspectives.

Origins: avoiding 'spurious orthodoxies'

The public funding of social science and humanities research in the UK is a product of the embrace of economic planning in the post-1945 decades. The so-called post-war consensus privileged the idea of state intervention, manifest in economic planning and welfare state programmes, as the means for managing modern societies. The same principle set the background for public social science funding and injected a distinct rationale into such public spending. In the articulation of this principle, however, there seemed to be a clear understanding of university researchers as professional members of a class in direct association with the political class of politicians and administrators. In other words, a common ethos might shape the direction of research in ways consistent with the needs of social and political objectives and their administration.

A year after the end of the war, in 1946, the Committee on the Provision for Social and Economic Research, chaired by Sir John Clapham, issued its report, strongly endorsing such state spending: 'it is a platitude that modern industrial communities rest on a knowledge of the subject matter of the natural sciences. It should be also a platitude that their smooth running and balance rest upon a knowledge of social needs and social responses' (Clapham Report 1946: 3). For example, the committee averred, economic policy could not be 'properly viewed without knowledge of economic quantities and economic institutions. In simpler societies it may have been safe to base social policies on hunch and traditional wisdom. But in more complex conditions such a basis it not enough' (Clapham Report 1946: 3). Reading as slightly naive about the straightforward meaning of 'social science knowledge', this first public review of public funding absorbed the idea that state finances should help scholarly research in social science, the products of which would benefit society. This role reflected wartime successes and a perceived alignment in elite opinion and wider public opinion about social purposes. The sociologist A.H. Halsey argues that at the end of the Second World War, state planning was viewed as an instrument of social improvement: 'by general consent a world fit for heroes and cripples was to be created, giving civilized substance to peace and justifying the sacrifices of war' (1994: 432).

However, while supportive of additional funding Clapham's committee did not recommend a dedicated research council, mainly because of reservations about how scientific social science could be. The Clapham Report stated: 'We believe that the parallelism which is suggested between the present needs of the social and natural sciences is ill-founded. The social sciences have not yet reached the stage at which such an official body could be brought into operation without danger of a premature crystallization of spurious orthodoxies' (1946: 12). In its report, the committee emphasized the value of data compilation for government in modern societies, a process that it believed could be reinforced with augmented funding. In respect of university funding, the Clapham committee recommended an increase in social science research funds over the coming years, administered by the University Grants Committee (UGC). Despite the caveat to avoid 'spurious orthodoxies' this recommendation for enhanced funding (which was acted upon) and the creation of a standing Interdepartmental Economic and Social Research Committee in Whitehall signalled greater state involvement in social science funding.

Founding a research council: 'long run utilitarian standards'

The pressure from universities and some government departments for greater investment in social and economic research and the creation of a specialist research council grew in the years after the Clapham Report appeared. Rhetoric about technology's importance, the value of planning and economic intervention became accepted as commonplace, and growing intellectual respect for social science fanned this trend.[3] The suitability of state-directed planning became a theme in David Glass's Inaugural Lecture as Professor of Sociology at the London School of Economics in 1950: 'I take it as axiomatic that planning even more in the social than in the economic field, is here to stay' (1950: 17). Glass advocated the need for a comprehensive research programme to ensure a firm basis for such public policy: 'the larger the area of governmental responsibility in the field of social policy, the greater the urgency for governmental action to be based on and tested by social research' (1950: 18). His proposals convey the intellectual and political mindset of post-war professional civil servants, public intellectuals, engaged politicians and academics about the likely dividends in terms of improved social and economic policy to follow from deeper empirical knowledge in society, demography and the economy. This view was widely held and fashioned a support network for the creation of a research council – eventually recommended by the Heyworth Committee in 1965. Support for greater social research extended into the private sector too, with the Heyworth Committee recording 'a remarkable amount of sympathy with the aims of the social sciences and an appreciation of the benefits to be anticipated from their application as shown by their demand for more' (Heyworth Report 1965: 28).

The Heyworth Committee issued a report recommending the establishment of a research council exclusively to fund social science in 1965. The road to this recommendation was lengthy and required overcoming doubts about how such social research could be judged.[4] Four types of issues shaped the committee members' articulation of the case for a social science council. First, opinion differed as to whether funded research should be measurably applied and utilitarian or supportive of individuals' own creative choices. Both types of research activity benefited in the long run. Second, the committee admired but could not hope to emulate the scale of American public investment in funding social science research. Third, engaging in predictive scientific analysis was to be limited. The committee members preferred applied empirical research and were doubtful about the capacity of social science to be scientifically predictive, and articulated a preference for middle-range hypothesis setting and testing rather than all-embracing integrated theory. This preference was a further differentiation from the United States where National Science Foundation funding of social science took the high road of theory building from the start of its funding (see Kleinman 1995; Larsen 1992). Last, the committee acknowledged a standard positivist model of social research, including training in statistical methods. The report adumbrated: 'it is essential that ... no student will in future graduate in the social sciences without a good working knowledge of statistics' (Heyworth Report 1965: 32).

Despite the general political context, which viewed social research as a tool of improved public policy-making including social amelioration, the Heyworth Committee sought to evaluate the validity of this precept. Opinion divided between those who wanted basic research funding unrelated to any policy application and those who stressed the importance of prioritizing applied research. The latter position was the majority one. Among the critics the London School of Economics sociologist Duncan MacRae (Committee on Social Studies 1964: 3) thought social theory separate from applied policy-making and problem-solving. Nuffield sociologist A.H. Halsey shared this view for different reasons – he wanted social scientists to be social critics, elaborating: 'I am very worried that our Social Science Council will too much represent that kind of legitimate [utilitarian] interest as over against the very much more difficult problem of inviting a society to have the nerve to build into its own establishment arrangements, arrangements for criticising its own establishment' (Committee on Social Studies 1964: 19–20). The importance of this argument has recurred ever since in discussion about the purpose and legitimacy of publicly funded social research. For instance, the Rothschild Enquiry recognized the need for social researchers at various points to have independence from political pressures to complete objective research.

The dominant view in discussions informing the Heyworth Committee's deliberations and report assumed that social research derived its value, and in many ways its legitimacy, from the potential to be applied in policy. Economist Alec Cairncross set out the utilitarian justification. He contended that 'social problems are meat and drink to the social scientist, they are what he is engaged in discussing'. Cairncross reduced this approach to two types of research activity: first, modelling social and economic forces to assist in the prediction of future developments, an activity justifying the label 'science'; and second, Cairncross and others argued that investigating the success and efficacy of government policy in achieving stated ends constituted crucial research. Combining theory and evidence was essential since, 'it is often a very bad thing if your theorists are cut off from application,' with an obvious danger of theoretical vacuity. For Cairncross what contemporary policy-makers call the 'impact' of research was a basic criterion of evaluation: 'you cannot absolve yourself from some kind of long-run utilitarian standard in the social sciences' (Committee on Social Studies Minutes 1964: 1, 3, 8–9). Committee member Noel Annan expected SSRC funding to enable a cadre of social science graduates 'educated in a particular technique of dealing with social problems' (Committee on Social Studies Minutes 1964: 18).

Topics singled out by the Heyworth Committee for detailed study under the rubric of applied research included: economic growth and development, including incomes policy, the application of science in industry and industrial efficiency; regional development; environmental issues including land use, planning and urban renewal; education; welfare; health; immigration; law and society; and international relations. Housing policy was cited as a prime candidate for applied investigation. The list is practical and policy-oriented. In sum, the Heyworth Committee's recommendation for a dedicated social research council and for educating publicly more researchers rested on a conception of social science research as primarily applied in character.

Based on the evidence submitted and solicited that the 'social sciences are ready to move to a new level of performance and for this they need funds for research on a larger scale' (Heyworth Report 1965: 47), the Heyworth Committee presented its recommendation for a Social Science Research Council. While there was increasing demand for the products of social research by users, the latter were unable to provide sufficient resources for substantial progress to be made; public funding was crucial. Social science research had become routinized in universities and the number and quality of researchers had expanded substantially. The report dismissed Clapham's fear of 'spurious orthodoxy': 'the considerable developments in the social sciences since the Clapham Committee have removed any dangers of the establishment of "spurious orthodoxies"' (Heyworth Report 1965: 46). A council would be able to monitor and direct research, ensuring that appropriate needs were addressed. In addition, an expansion in funding of postgraduate studentships was recommended. Both proposals were enacted.

Set up under the Science and Technology Act 1965, the Social Science Research Council reflected the values dominating the Heyworth Committee's assessment of social science, in particular the assumption that research could produce information and valid relationships between policies and effects or outcomes usable in public policy. Its remit was to fund research activity by scholars in universities and to allocate studentships for advanced training in the social sciences. The disciplines it covered were sociology, human geography, social anthropology, economics, social statistics, economic history, political science (later international relations, too), and some parts of psychology and law. Organizationally the council had a set of senior administrative staff and a set of committees covering the disciplines and particular tasks, which were staffed by academics from universities and some senior researchers. Decisions about grant allocation and studentship awards rested on anonymous peer review, the evaluations of which were considered and adjudicated on by the relevant council committee. This structure remains largely in place, although there is now a chief executive appointed for five years at a time. There is also an advisory board.

Surviving a challenge: 'an act of intellectual vandalism'

Aside from continuing struggles to maintain its annual budget to fund research and graduate studentships, the biggest crisis for the ESRC followed the election of the Conservative Party to government in 1979 under the leadership of the New Right figure, Mrs Margaret Thatcher. The forewarning from Halsey that a social research council might acquire the role of engaging in institutionalized criticism seemed to have arrived. Several intellectual luminaries in the Conservative Party doubted the value or even possibility of social research (particularly if was called a 'science') and through their own think-tanks, notably the Institute of Economic Affairs, expanded and promoted economic ideas such as monetarism out of favour with the prevailing Keynesian consensus supported by the research council (Crockett 1994).

Amongst the new Prime Minister's inner circle, her Education Secretary Sir Keith Joseph was doubtful about a publicly funded commitment to social science,[5] although he was far from uninterested in the types of research projects and questions social scientists addressed. He was sceptical about the term scientific and the resources needed. To assess the council's value and necessity he commissioned a distinguished natural scientist, Lord Rothschild, to review the work of the SSRC.[6] The appointment was in December 1981 and Rothschild completed and published the results of his enquiry in May 1982. The parameters of the enquiry were to assess the extent to which a research council was required and able to identify top research projects, the best way of undertaking that research and what means would best address the questions posed.[7] Rothschild consulted widely with leading academics in social science, citing their opinions and judgements in his report. These were almost uniformly positive about social science and the role of the SSRC in facilitating social research.

Rothschild himself reported favourably about the SSRC. In fact, his report concluded in ways entirely the obverse of the perceived views of the Education Secretary and Conservative government. Rothschild declared, 'there is one course of action which could not be easily corrected: that is the dismemberment or liquidation of the SSRC. That would not only be an act of intellectual vandalism ... it would also have damaging consequences for the whole country' (Rothschild Report 1982: para. 11.19). In other words the evidence and arguments that led the Clapham and Heyworth committees to recommend expanded public funding of social science research were vindicated in the quality of research Rothschild encountered and in the appropriateness of research questions investigated under SSRC funding. And those earlier reports' support for expanded graduate studentship programmes was also supported by Lord Rothschild. He wanted a steady state in the council's annual spending allocation to give its administrators stability to plan and fund research appropriately.[8] Finally, as a natural scientist Lord Rothschild proved fully able to assess and justify the scientific status of social science research as plausible and well adhered to in best practice research projects.

A month after its publication, the Rothschild Report was the subject of a debate in the House of Lords initiated by Lord Max Beloff, the Oxford academic. Previously a critic of the research council (notably in his views about the Warwick Industrial Relations Research Unit),[9] he now accepted, in the light of Rothschild's conclusions, that the council merited supported and continued existence. Beloff explained:

> First, that while the social sciences are a particularly difficult and sensitive area of research because of their political and social connotations, they nevertheless deserve a measure of public support, for the same reason as public support is sought for the natural sciences or for the humanities; that is to say, because there are certain forms of addition to our knowledge, to our treasures of information, which it is right for the state to support.

He continued, that on the basis of the report, 'while far from perfect, the Social Science Research Council is probably, or could be if reformed, as good a single instrument for supporting such research as it is likely one could devise; and the only alternative, which is not fully considered in the report, would be wider dissemination of public money to universities, to learned societies in the field, and so forth.'[10] Indeed Rothschild's report gave the SSRC, in the words of this fellow peer, 'a fairly clean bill of health'.[11]

Rothschild was highly supportive of government funding for research in the social sciences (and for such funding to be orchestrated under the SSRC). He argued first that certain disciplines, such as social anthropology, would perish without such research support: 'they are peculiarly dependent upon governmental support through Research Councils, and their results and their methods are of great interest to a number of disciplines, both practical and theoretical.' The continuing and vital need for empirical research, based on 'high academic standards', to inform major public policy decisions was a further reason for state funding of research. Rothschild was healthily sceptical of the precarious knowledge base upon which much 'entrenched common sense' commonly rested. Finally, Rothschild judged that the absence of publicly funded research findings would in practice overwhelm the users of such research bereft of intellectual and monetary resources to undertake the necessary research: it would 'impose a burden on 'consumer' departments and agencies which they could not sustain' (Rothschild Report 1982: 21).

The name of the research council changed to its present-day Economic and Social Research Council. This modification came some months after the delivery of the Rothschild Report, as the Education Secretary accepted the findings not to dismember the council but achieved a symbolic victory in getting 'science' excised from its title. This change was a modest price to pay for the council's defenders and beneficiaries who had known that the prospect of abolition was real.

The Rothschild Report is thirty years old. The research council's survival of this challenge put an end to any serious consideration of the ESRC's abolition (even in the current era of no-holds-barred austerity measures). Its role as a public agency required to respond to social and economic trends through purposeful research funding (including subsequently greater use of directed research programmes) was secured; and the legitimacy of increasing the number of postgraduate-educated social scientists in the UK – an ambition of both the Clapham and Heyworth reports – was affirmed. Both of these facets – that some social research should be publicly underwritten because of the inherent nature of the activity and that education be expanded – withstood therefore the challenge of New Right neo-liberal economic arguments which gained prominence first under the monetarist-inspired deregulatory and anti-state revolution initiated by Mrs Thatcher, and also withstood the end of the Cold War, the outcome of which had constituted a victory for anti-statism and free-market economics. The scale of this achievement has perhaps been insufficiently remarked upon: born as a handmaiden of a Keynesian-dominated, post-war consensus, the country's social science research council managed to retain its legitimacy and purpose in the very different post-1970s world of neo-liberal, pro-market and anti-public spending politics. And this account is not intended to imply that the SSRC/ESRC ever had an especially easy time of negotiating annual allocations for research or graduate studentships. For instance, in the fiscal year 1981/82, 880 postgraduate studentships were awarded, 50 per cent below the allocation three years earlier (ESRC 2005: 24).

The ESRC after Rothschild

The ESRC faced tough times in the first half of the 1980s as budgets were tight and the aura of having been challenged by the government endured. From the middle of the decades it consolidated. Three aspects of that consolidation bearing noting.

The integration of research and government policy

One theme developed in the Rothschild Report was the desirability of enhanced connections between industry and social research to ensure, as he saw it, that social research had some sensitivity to the needs of employers and industrialists. This motif was present in both the Clapham and Heyworth committee reports, though more so in the former. It is a theme that has reverberated and increased since the 1980s. And in an early formulation of what has become the notion of 'users', Rothschild talked about the 'ultimate customer' or consumer of social research financed through a publicly funded council. Whereas Rothschild argued that the consumer of applied research was enormously widely spread – from policy-makers through to the media and general public – the idea of the user has become a narrower one in subsequent research council practice. It is presented as widely based but, unless researchers are fortunate enough to get their results presented in a documentary or other mass media format, informing the general public as user is hard. Lord Ardwick, a former administrator at the Nuffield Foundation, summarized this view:

The social science customer includes all those who have a part to play in The decision-making process. The decisions to which most of the research sponsored by the council contributes are essentially governmental. But in a democratic society these decisions are not the sole concerns of Ministers or officials. The beneficiaries of this applied research are Members of Parliament, journalists, academics and the public at large. There is no single customer who might take out a contract. So though much research may still be commissioned by such customers as Government departments and private organizations, the public interest requires, Lord Rothschild says, an independent source of funds for research which such customers cannot be expected to undertake.[12]

The parallel here with the reincarnations through which the idea of measuring public significance of academic research has gone – now called 'impact' – in the RAE/REF exercise is salutary. From a modest origin this notion of impact will constitute the basis for 25 per cent of awards in the 2014 assessment exercise and subject panels have been bolstered with members deemed non-academic users able to drive the impact judgement. While the need to identify research users and research impact both constitute strategies to make certain aspects of public spending politically palatable, the effects of such initiatives bear wider reflection.

Various important initiatives occurred in the ESRC in the 1980s and 1990s. The idea of dedicated research centres began with the council funding initially and then the host university picking it up. The work of the Centre for Ethnic Studies at Warwick and Centre for African Economics at Oxford are notable achievements. But the council also moved more towards thematic research programmes, allocating funds for large research initiatives funded by programme directors seconded from their normal university position. While not the sole activity of the council by any means, organizing research allocations and other activities in terms of such themes or challenges acquired greater significance. By 2011 these were termed strategic priorities, the three of which were identified above. In the previous strategic plan these were called challenge areas including: New Technology and Skills; Global Economic Performance, Policy and Management; and Global Uncertainties.

Publicizing the findings

To address the recurrent issue of failing sufficiently to publicize and explain its activities – a role both Heyworth and Rothschild underlined – the ESRC has a public engagement programme including periodic Festivals of Social Science and publicizing the results of its funded research.

Professionalizing postgraduate training

The SSRC-ESRC has played a key role in advancing research training for postgraduates in the UK. From the early 1990s the ESRC introduced Postgraduate Training Requirements which imposed rules and expectations on university studentships, supervisors and students. These and subsequent measures align the research council with a quantitative and positivist view of the discipline, increasingly so over time, as ESRC recognition came to be seen as a 'kite-mark' for doctoral programmes and most universities sought recognition for all their departments offering social science PhDs.

Such a stance is entirely consistent with the expectations of the authors of the Clapham, Heyworth and Rothschild reports that postgraduate studentships should train graduate students as social scientists. This emphasis has certainly not meant the neglect of qualitative subjects such as international relations or social anthropology, although proponents of these disciplines have often felt such oversight; and many supervisors have blanched at the training requirements imposed uniformly on recipients of graduate studentships regardless of the student's methodology or research topic. Even more resented in some universities is the diffusion of ESRC postgraduate training standards as the norm for all graduates on courses winning the coveted ESRC training recognition award. In my view this objection is entirely misplaced as the benefits of proper training in research methods and professional skills has hugely benefited the standard of graduate provision in the affected disciplines.

The establishment of Doctoral Training Centres (DTCs) from 2012, however, marks a modification of this development. Whereas there was a significant degree of concentration in the distribution of awards to recognized departments through the studentship competition, the anticipation of cuts to funding led the ESRC to abandon the competition in favour of quota awards assigned to DTCs (involving some forty-two universities, some in collaborative arrangements with neighbouring universities, to form twenty-one DTCs in all). The other universities, who were previously recognized, have lost recognition.

In fact, this policy outcome appears consistent with government policies for concentration and selectivity in research across the sector and will further the tendency to create a hierarchy of universities, with a limited number of research-intensive universities at the top. This 'hierarchization' is linked to the policy of differential fees for undergraduate programmes, and the removal of the teaching block grant from arts, humanities and social sciences. Student choice will determine the distribution of subjects available at universities. To the extent that social sciences are perceived as priority subjects, it is through their role of augmenting undergraduates and postgraduates competence in quantitative methods (see MacInnes 2009). In terms of postgraduate research, it is significant that HEFCE is now undertaking a consultation on the distribution of the quality-related research (QR) element of funding associated with postgraduate research (the equivalent of the undergraduate teaching block grant and worth about a similar amount, i.e. making up half the income a university received for postgraduate home research students). The terms of the consultation suggest the concentration of postgraduate QR funding in fewer universities.

Fiscal crisis and social research: the imperative to 'to broaden and accelerate'

The Great Recession (2007–8) and its continuing effects – with an expected lack of economic growth for ten years in the worst affected advanced democracies – have two key implications for a public research regime. First, they reaffirm the urgency of publicly funding researchers and new graduate students in the key disciplines that attempt to understand the causes, processes, outcomes and long-term effects of such exogenous shocks to stable democracies. But, second, they underline the need for a research council to expand its openness to innovative research projects designed to understand both the present malaise and pending black swans. 'Innovative' does not simply mean interdisciplinary (though there should be more of that, for example, combining economic history and sociology), nor embracing some current fashionable turn (such as behavioural or experimental economics, the results of which often give new meaning to the blindingly obvious). Rather, it means recognizing a plurality of research projects targeted on a set of problems thrown up by the Great Recession (public sector versus private sector conflicts, money and politics, regulatory regimes and income inequality trends, for instance), and the value of posing large themes and explanatory factors such as those associated with political economy and political institutions.

This kind of thematically rich and intellectually deep research and analysis perfectly complements and interacts with the kind of applied research already undertaken by the research council funded scholars and anticipated in the Clapham and Heyworth reports. But we need both types.[13] And for the reasons Rothschild celebrated in his report – only an independent research agency can be expected to fund research which may produce politically unpalatable findings – the university community must insist that the ESRC continues to take a broad-stroke view of research activity and is not only overly harnessed to any particular agenda. Thus, in terms of the historical debate about whether public research councils should fund merely applied or pure research, the latter should retain equal weight in the allocation of resources. It is exactly this view that explains the financial investor George Soros' funding of the Institute for New Economics Thinking (INET). Through its research funding the institute promises to 'broaden and accelerate the development of new economic thinking that can lead to solutions for the great challenges of the twentieth first century'.[14]

Thus, ironically, while many politicians may view the present scale of the fiscal crisis of the state as the moment to view public funding of social science research as an unaffordable luxury, it is in fact precisely the occasion when we most need to secure and fund our national community of researchers. Publicly funded research is an important and necessary function of the public university.

6

The Religion of Inequality

Stephen McKay and Karen Rowlingson

This chapter considers the relationship between higher education, equal opportunities and unequal outcomes. It also places the reduction of public spending on universities in the wider context of cuts to welfare benefits and the protection of wealth. We argue that the direction of reform is towards changes that reinforce, if not extend, existing inequalities and which reduce the opportunities available to lower income groups. These changes, whatever the rhetoric of fairness, represent an erosion of social rights.

A crisis that was born of poor regulation of free markets in finance is leading to the reassertion of the power of markets, and their great extension to higher education. Tawney's work of 1931 that provides this chapter's title is particularly prescient, in that he talks of the British tolerance for 'a handful of bankers to raise and lower the economic temperature of a whole community' (1964: 41 [1931]). He also enquires whether the system of inequality that Matthew Arnold saw as inevitably breaking down in the long run had yet to run its course – and certainly the optimism that was present between the 1930s and 1960s must now confront a reality of very persistent inequalities that have been reasserting themselves since the mid-1970s. The education system plays a key role here, with unequal educational outcomes being both a cause and a consequence of economic inequality. Dorling has also argued recently that the view that elitism is efficient, and that relatively few may gain from advanced education, helps to perpetuate inequality and is one of his five 'tenets of injustice' (2010: 1).

Under the current set of public policy reforms those who might previously have been labelled as citizens are instead consumers of services. Higher education may be further along that road than some other policy areas, as a result of the Browne Report and its implementation, but this is the route being well-travelled in other public policy developments. These new policies aim, not at the abatement of class differentials, but at ensuring their importance and their continuation. Among other areas, this may be seen in the current proposals for legal aid and in child maintenance, where consultations are ongoing but the direction of reform seems set. The clear aim in each case is to remove the state as an important player, and rely on solutions being negotiated at a personal level or through exclusively private-sector solutions, leaving clear inequalities in negotiating power. The UK and other liberal economies have already been facing a decline in social cohesion and social trust, which Green, Janmaat and Cheng (2011) attribute to a declining faith in the working of a meritocratic society.

We also look at attitudes towards higher education, using data from various waves of the British Social Attitudes Survey, to demonstrate that what people expect from higher education is at odds with the direction of reform. People believe that opportunities to participate in higher education should be expanded and, if tuition fees are to exist at all, they should be the same for all institutions – in other words not a market with price-based competition. We also show the earnings and occupational status differentials that accrue to graduates. These remain high, compared to those gaining lower qualifications. This set of results is based on new analysis of the latest data from the Labour Force Survey in 2010.

Trends in inequality

Levels of inequality of incomes and especially of top earnings have been growing for some time in the UK, and in many other nations. Whilst Marshall was able to point to the 'compression, at both ends, of the scale of income distribution' (1992 [1950]: 44), as being a positive force for welfare state development (via social rights), the more recent picture is of the very top of the income distribution moving further away from those near the top, who in turn are moving away from the middle. The reduction in inequality being observed in the 1950s and before in fact did continue for some time, and between 1961 and 1979 incomes increased throughout the income distribution. Indeed, those at the poorer end of the distribution experienced the fastest income growth, leading to a reduction in inequality of incomes.

This pattern turned around after 1979. Between 1979 and 1995 incomes rose most quickly at the upper end of the income distribution, with only limited increases for those on lower incomes. The richest tenth saw their real incomes (i.e. after adjusting for inflation) rise by 60 per cent while the poorest tenth saw only a 10 per cent rise. Hills has encapsulated these trends up to the mid-1990s: 'the poor fell behind the middle; the middle fell behind the top; and the top fell behind the very top' (2004: 25–6). In the following decade, New Labour pursued a policy of greater redistribution towards lower income households, and particularly those with children. The economic conditions also supported a greater movement into paid work of some poorer groups, in particular lone parents and older workers who had relatively low rates of labour force participation. These trends contributed towards some uplift in the incomes of the poorest groups, and some small but hard-won reductions in poverty. Nevertheless, it was not an explicit part of policy to tackle overall inequality or the dramatic increase in the highest incomes, even where this was attracting considerable public concern (McKay and Rowlingson 2008). Hills' interpretation of changes to the income distribution during this period (up to around 2004) is of 'the poor catching up on the middle to some extent, but the top moving away from the middle' (2004: 26).

Subsequent policy did not really change this picture (Stewart 2009). In the last few years of the New Labour government there was lesser new investment in transfers to lower income families, and child poverty again began to increase.

In the most recent accounts of the development of greater inequality, the top of the income distribution is described as moving away from the rest, and in particular the movement of the very top of the distribution is significant. In Figure 6.1 we focus on some of the highest incomes, and show the share of income received by the top 1 per cent of individuals for each year between 1950 and 2000. What Marshall (lecturing in 1949) perceived as a compression at the top was actually gaining pace with a large reduction in the income of this group between 1950 and 1960, and a further large fall in their share of overall incomes in the early 1970s. In 1950 some 13 per cent of total income was accounted for by the top 1 per cent of income earners. This fell back to a low of 6.5 per cent in 1978, only to again return to the level of 13 per cent by the year 2000.

THE RELIGION OF INEQUALITY 93

Figure 6.1 Share of total incomes received by the top 1 per cent, 1950-2000
Source: Leigh 2007. UK data drawn from Atkinson 2007

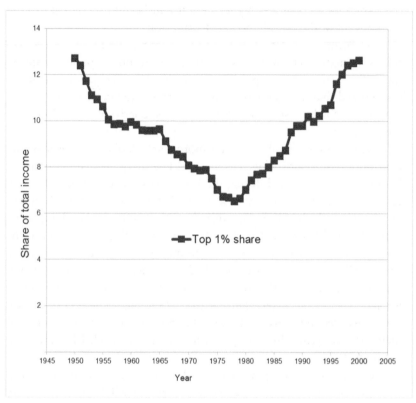

As with wider trends in income distribution, the 1980s stand out as being associated with rapid increases in inequality and the level of rewards at the top. This concentration of incomes continued during the 1990s, and was only slowed (rather than halted or reversed) in the first years of the New Labour government. Overall, therefore, the income share of the top 1 per cent of earners in Britain was broadly the same in the year 2000 as it had been in 1950.

Beyond the top 1 per cent there is evidence of even greater concentration of incomes. Atkinson and Salverda (Atkinson and Salverda 2003) have used records of income tax to examine the incomes of those at the very top of the earnings distribution (and known to the tax authorities). They investigate trends among the very top 0.05 per cent (broadly, the 'top ten thousand'). Their share of income fell between the mid-1920s and mid-1970s – very much in line with the fortunes of the top 1 per cent. However, their incomes have rebounded to such an extent that by 1997 their share of income was higher than it had been in 1937 – at around 2.4 per cent of the overall income distribution.

In 2010, the new National Equality Panel reported that the UK had relatively high levels of inequality compared to other countries, and in the 1980s saw a more rapid increase in levels of income inequality. It emphasized that it was the pattern at the top of the income distribution that was mostly responsible for the UK's relatively high degree of inequality.

There have been similar, perhaps more marked, trends in the changing distribution of wealth, as well as income. The sharp inequalities of asset-holding were challenged during the first three-quarters of the twentieth century, some of which may be attributed to the effects of death duties, but much of which reflected a redistribution of assets within the wealthy (Atkinson and Harrison 1978). In 1923, the wealthiest 1 per cent of the population owned 61 per cent of the marketable assets. By the more equal 1970s, this had fallen to only 21 per cent of the assets – but it was still the case that the top 10 per cent of wealth-holders accounted for half the overall assets. During the 1990s this reduction in wealth inequality went into reverse. From 1988–99, the top 1 per cent increased their share of wealth from 17 per cent to 23 per cent (HM Revenue and Customs 2011).

The inequalities of pay mentioned above are also found *within* universities. At our own research-intensive Russell Group University (the University of Birmingham), annual accounts show that the number of staff (other than the vice-chancellor) earning in excess of £100,000 rose from thirty-two people in 2001–2 to ninety-six people by 2009–10. Figures for Reading University, a member of the 1994 Group, show a rise over the same period from just one person to twenty-two people in the most recent figures. University College London has over 300 people receiving such salaries. The increased remuneration levels of vice-chancellors have already been documented, and appear to have only a limited association with institutional performance (Baimbridge and Simpson 1996; Tarbert, Tee and Watson 2008). Instead vice-chancellors' earnings seem to be driven by the level of pay being given elsewhere in the university (differentials), the size of remuneration being offered to other vice-chancellors and to changes in the compensation of chief executives in the private sector (Tarbert *et al.* 2008).

These figures describe very high levels of inequality. However, we might also consider whether these differences are the result of fair opportunities. If all people have a more or less equal chance of getting on in life, rather than life chances being determined at birth, then there is a case to be argued that the inequalities we observed may be fair. Certainly, the political parties are mindful of low rates of social mobility and their deleterious effects, and apt to promote the concept of equality of opportunities rather than of outcomes. This is very clear in the policies and speeches of Prime Minsters Blair and Brown. Even within the coalition government we may see the same concern for opportunities – and the same disdain for merely looking at simple figures on the inequality of income or wealth. Nick Clegg, the Deputy Prime Minister and the leader of the Liberal Democrats, said that, 'Social mobility is what characterises a fair society, rather than a particular level of income inequality. Inequalities become injustices when they are fixed: passed on, generation to generation' (Clegg 2010). We look at some inter-generational features, below. However, there is strong evidence that inequalities are relatively fixed and are passed on.

The research evidence on social mobility shows clearly that we do not live in a perfectly meritocratic society: people's occupational and economic destinations depend to an important degree on their origins (Blanden, Gregg and Machin 2005; Blanden and Machin 2007; Breen and Goldthorpe 1999; Goldthorpe and Mills 2008; Iannelli and Paterson 2006; McKay 2010; Macmillan 2009; National Equality Panel 2010; Nicoletti and Ermisch 2007). And if we compare Britain with other countries, rates of intergenerational mobility in terms of incomes are low and in terms of occupation are below the international average for men and at the bottom of the range for women. Blanden (Blanden 2009) has shown that social mobility is lower in societies which are more unequal. Britain, the United States and Brazil had the lowest levels of social mobility in terms of income. It therefore seems to matter more in Britain who your parents are than in many other countries.

Parents matter because they pass on a range of forms of capital to their children: social; cultural; and human. They also, crucially, pass on substantial economic capital, in relation to lifetime gifts (some of which may directly help their children through higher education) and in relation to inheritance, which continues to make up a high proportion of wealth inequality – particularly at the higher end. The middle classes are most likely to receive both inheritances and lifetime gifts, and the most likely to receive high-valued inheritances and lifetime gifts (Rowlingson and McKay 2005).

Parents often pass capital on to their children and this can fuel intra-generational inequality between families with substantial resources and those without. But there is also inter-generational inequality. For example in *The Pinch*, Willetts (2010) argued that different birth cohorts have had very different fates, in terms of opportunities to accumulate wealth, acquire pensions and enjoy stable employment. In particular, he argues that the post-war 'baby boom' generation (those born in 1945–65) have enjoyed unusually favourable economic and other conditions (including consumption, wealth and the 'best music') tantamount to having taken the future from younger age groups. It is just those younger age groups that are now facing the brave new world of market-level university tuition fees. Willetts, the current Minister of State for Universities and Science, argues that means have to be found of reducing the level of inter-cohort inequality, but of course the introduction of market-level fees in a higher education free market runs counter to that aspiration. This does look like the baby boomers – beneficiaries of free higher education – pulling up the ladder behind them.

Higher education policy, equal opportunities and unequal outcomes

Until the 1960s, universities were elite institutions, open to only a small percentage of the population. The expansion of higher education (at the same time as decreasing inequality – perhaps no coincidence) led to many more middle-class and even some working-class young people going to university. But the number began to stagnate in the 1980s and Britain fell behind many other countries leading to a further push to expand higher education and also widen access. Part of the aim of this expansion and widening access was to increase equal opportunities. The proportion going to university has certainly increased since the 1980s but the proportion coming from poorer backgrounds has changed very little. But even with this expansion, the UK still lags behind many of its competitors (and future competitors) in relation to graduate numbers. According to the Organisation for Economic Co-operation and Development (2007: 2), 'the proportion of the UK's age cohort entering tertiary-type A programmes ... in 2005 ... was 51%, compared to an

OECD average of 54% ... In Australia, Finland, Hungary, Iceland, New Zealand, Norway, Poland, Sweden and the United States more than 60% of young people will enter tertiary-type A programmes.'

It is not hard to understand why many countries are increasing the proportion of their young people that they put through tertiary education. The future of work, as outlined in Reich (1991) is likely to include increasing returns to professional skills and knowledge, as those with these talents are able to seek employment in a range of different national and global markets. Routine production work, by contrast, is likely to move to those countries with the lowest costs and often that will mean the places with the lowest wages. In-service workers are less at risk from international competition, though migration may act as a downward force on wages. But their situation will depend on the success of the more skilled workforce. Many countries are therefore pursuing a strategy of high skills in the workforce, and high value added to the production chain. In Finland and South Korea, participation rates in higher education are around the 70 per cent level, far in excess of the UK.

But why has the 'widening access' agenda had such little success? Perhaps one of the reasons is that fear of indebtedness varies by social class, and thus has different effects on lower income socioeconomic groups. Pennell and West (Pennell and West 2005) argued that those from poorer backgrounds also tend to graduate with the highest levels of debt. Having an aversion to debt reduces the propensity to attend university. The strategy of working part-time whilst studying may help to reduce the final debt, but may be associated with a lower level of attainment (Purnell and West 2005). Other research has suggested that lower-income students are more likely than others to perceive tuition fees as constituting debt rather than any kind of investment (Callender and Jackson 2008). The research also found that those from lower socioeconomic groups tended to modify their choice of institution (though not of subject) to select somewhere with lower living costs and greater opportunities for part-time paid work. Many students are also encouraged to seek a local university in the interests of keeping down costs (Mangan *et al* 2010), including quite high-achieving students whose chances of going to a 'good' university depend on whether there is one available to them locally. The policy of having bursaries and other forms of support directed at low income families is a tacit acknowledgement that fees may be a deterrent to some people attending university, despite the insistence that the lack of upfront costs means there should be no financial impediment to going to university among such groups.

While numbers of graduates have been increasing in the UK, particularly among the middle classes, a university degree remains associated with a significant wage premium. It is just this kind of pecuniary advantage that the Browne Report was so keen to emphasize. There is a strong association between higher hourly pay, and having a degree, as we now show. These results are taken from the quarterly Labour Force Survey for July-September 2010,[1] the most recent data available. With the economy still struggling to recover, they may provide a relatively cautious picture of graduate earnings. In Figure 6.2 we compare the median[2] hourly pay of those with degrees, with those who have A levels or the equivalent. There are other relevant groups – such as those with non-degree higher education leading to diplomas, but these two groups provide a clear comparison.

The first point to notice is that, aside from those aged 21–24, graduates earn considerably more than those with A-level qualifications. Among those aged 30–34, for instance, graduates were earning an average of £16 per hour (around £33,000 per year for a standard working week), compared with £10 per hour for those with A-level qualifications (around

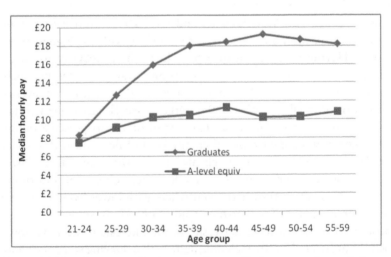

Figure 6.2 Hourly pay (median) among those with degrees or the equivalent of A levels

Source: Office for National Statistics, Social and Vital Statistics Division and Northern Ireland Statistics and Research Agency, Central Survey Unit 2010

£21,000 per year). The second key point is that this gap enjoyed by graduates tends to increase at least until people are in their forties. If we just looked at pay differentials at an early age – as happens with studies of the destinations of leavers from higher education – we are liable to understate the advantages of having achieved a degree. Having a degree may not lead to higher earnings in the first few years after graduation, when those with A levels will have accumulated several more years of work experience, but increasingly may do so at older ages. The age-earnings profile of those with A levels (and indeed lesser qualifications) is relatively flat. For graduates average earnings do not peak until well into the working lifetime. There are therefore likely to be rewards for those able to postpone gratification – either in terms of attitudes or being able to rely on support from their families.

Whilst we should be cautious about inferring lifecycle patterns from cross-sectional data, these different earnings trajectories – rising for graduates, relatively flat for those with A levels – are likely to be reflecting entry to professional careers with reliable pay progression. The professions are dominated by those with degrees, and most graduates reach either higher managerial/professional or lower managerial/ professional occupations, certainly once older than the age of twenty-five. Willetts even suggests that a degree is a 'rite of passage taking you into the middle class' (2010: 206). We show some further comparative figures in Table 6.1, again from the Labour Force Survey. This shows the proportions of different age groups who are in a professional or managerial occupation (both higher and lower, using the National Statistics Socio-Economic Classification, NS-SEC), separately for graduates and those with A levels or similar qualifications. Among those in work, and classified as being in a higher managerial or professional occupation, some 61 per cent have a degree, and a further 12 per cent received higher education but below degree standard. Only 13 per cent have only A-level standard qualifications, with relatively few with any qualifications below this standard reaching the NS-SEC classification of higher status.

To add to the inequalities generated from having a degree, over time private schools have become much more effective in gaining access to university places. Such schools have cemented their position, and their own increased fees, by taking an increasing share of graduate places relative to state schools. In research based on the 1958 and 1970 birth cohorts, Green et al. (2010) looked at the percentages of survey

Table 6.1 Class outcomes (NS-SEC) by age group and qualifications (%)

	Age group					
	21–24	25–29	30–34	35–39	40–44	45–49
Graduates						
Higher managerial and professional	11	27	36	39	42	39
Lower managerial and professional	37	45	45	44	42	44
Total:	48	72	81	83	83	83
Sample size	775	1,709	1,999	1,999	1,733	1,633
With A-levels (or equivalent)						
Higher managerial and professional	3	5	10	8	10	11
Lower managerial and professional	17	22	26	28	27	28
Total:	20	27	36	36	37	39
Sample size	904	1,185	1,152	1,239	1,499	1,486

Source: Office for National Statistics, Social and Vital Statistics Division and Northern Ireland Statistics and Research Agency, Central Survey Unit 2010

respondents gaining a first degree by the age of twenty-three. For those born in 1958, 41 per cent of those from private schools gained a degree, compared with 16 per cent of those from state schools. Those born in 1970 were able to benefit from the general expansion of higher expansion between these two cohorts. However, for those born in 1970, 59 per cent of those from private schools gained a degree (a rise of 18 percentage points for those from fee-paying schools) compared with 19 per cent of those from state schools (a rise of only 3 percentage points).

Social attitudes towards access to higher education

So what do the public think about higher education? Do they think that the expansion has gone far enough? Do they think that 'elitism is efficient' and that relatively few may gain from higher education? Or do they think that the government should do more to widen access? In Great Britain, since 1983 the British Social Attitudes Survey (BSAS) has taken the pulse of the people on a wide range of issues, by asking a long series of attitudinal questions. These have covered such diverse topics as priorities for government spending, the distribution of income and attitudes to divorce. In a few instances this valuable series of surveys has asked people for their attitudes towards higher education – should access be made tougher or easier, and views about tuition fees.

In many years of the BSAS series, people have been asked if they think that opportunities for higher education for young people should be expanded or restricted, and their views are depicted in . Clearly there was a significant turnaround in views during 2003–4 (when legislation was passed moving fees to a maximum of £3,000 per year). This led to a drop in the proportion wanting to increase opportunities for higher education, although numbers in favour have been slowly climbing up since then. Despite that particular change, it remained the case even in 2007 that 41 per cent of people thought that opportunities for young people to go on to higher education should be increased, whilst only 13 per cent thought they should be reduced. Many people (45 per cent) believed that opportunities to enter higher education, under the previous fees regime, were 'about right'.[3] There is no evidence that the general public believe that universities should be more elite and exclusive, with the vast majority of people (some 86 per cent) suggesting that such opportunities should either be increased, or are already at the right level (in 2007, at least).

To this general support for expanding opportunities to undertake higher education, we may add an important interest in social mobility. This has become a topic of increasing importance, with New Labour expressing particular concern about widening access to professional careers (Milburn 2009), and in particular in the light of the introduction of university fees at around £3,000 per annum (Langlands 2005). Even before such policy interest, the 2003 BSAS questionnaire asked how important it was that more people from a *working-class* background went to university. Overall 36 per cent described this as very important,

Figure 6.3 Do you feel that opportunities for young people in Britain to go on to higher education – to a university or college – should be increased or reduced, or are they at about the right level now? (1983–2007)
Source: National Centre for Social Research (1983–2007)

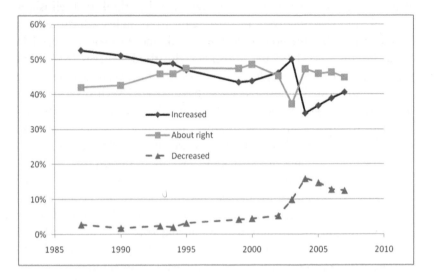

and a further 42 per cent as fairly important. Few thought that this was an unimportant feature to pursue.

In 2004, anticipating the change to the fees regime, respondents to the British Social Attitudes Survey were asked if tuition fees should vary either by subject or by university. The essence of a market in higher education, as promoted by the Browne Report, is that universities should be able to set different fees so that students face a differentiated choice. In 2004 (Table 6.2), however, two-thirds of respondents thought that fees should *not* vary by university, but should be the same for all. There was greater support (43 per cent), though still only a minority, for the idea that university tuition fees should vary according to the subject being studied. Overall, however, people believed that tuition fees should be the same regardless of the university a person attended, and almost as strongly that the subject chosen by students should not make a difference to the level of fees paid.

In 2005, there was a general view that the employment prospects for graduates had worsened compared to ten years previously. Half the respondents (50 per cent) believed that job prospects had worsened compared to around one-quarter (26 per cent) who thought that

Table 6.2 Attitudes towards variable university fees

Views on variations in tuition fees	Should tuition fees for all universities and colleges should be the same, or, different depending on the university students go to?	Should tuition fees be the same for all subjects studied, or different depending on the subject students study?
Should be the same	65	54
Should be different	32	43
Don't know	3	3
Sample size	3,200	3,200

Source: National Centre for Social Research (2004)

graduates now had better prospects, and slightly fewer (23 per cent) believing that they had not really changed much. In the same year, there were more mixed views about how the quality of teaching had changed. Whilst half thought that the standard of teaching was about the same as a decade ago, 28 per cent perceived that it had improved whilst 19 per cent detected that it had worsened. There is certainly no evidence of any general view that university teaching quality had worsened, despite declines in the average level of state support for teaching. Answers to this question were also relatively similar in 1999, conversely indicating no perceived change in teaching quality following the introduction of student fees.

Next we consider views about the overall role of university, and its effects on students. Three questions are analysed in Table 6.3. A strong majority of people (70 per cent) think that the advantages to going to university cannot simply be that of being paid more – with only seven per cent disagreeing. Some three-quarters (75 per cent) however believed that the costs of going to university – and at the time the maximum fee level was £3,000 per year – left students with debts that they were unable to afford to repay. Despite these views, a narrow majority (51 per cent) thought that those attending university would, at least in the long run, be a lot better off financially than those who did not attend university, with 18 per cent disagreeing that this would be the case.

Table 6.3 Views about university

Views on the effects of university	There are more advantages to a university education than simply being paid more	The cost of going to university leaves many students with debts that they can't afford to repay	In the long run people who go to university end up being a lot better off financially than those who don't
Strongly agree	14	19	8
Agree	56	56	43
Neither agree/ disagree	20	13	26
Disagree	6	9	17
Strongly disagree	1	*	1
Can't choose	3	2	3
Sample size	1,786	1,787	1,786

Note: * indicates less than 0.5 per cent but more than zero
Source: National Centre for Social Research (2005)

How might we sum up these views? This overall set of attitude questions confirms that British people are still committed to an increase in the opportunities to attend university, and in particular that more people from working-class backgrounds should attend. Whilst they generally acknowledge that a higher salary will result from attending university, very few see that as the main benefit of gaining a degree. Despite the continued expectation that graduates will be better off financially, albeit with a general reduction in their prospects over time, people still believe that many students will be left with large debts that they will be unable to afford. In terms of creating a market in higher education, most people think that all universities should be charging the same – a view that universities seem to share, at least as reflected in their past behaviour in setting fees. There is even a majority opposing the levying of different fees according to the subject being studied. In almost all cases these views are seriously at variance with the current direction of policy following the Browne Report – which emphasized the

Table 6.4 Views about equal opportunities

Per cent agreeing that ...	
... children from better-off families have many more opportunities than children from less well-off families	80
... some people have higher incomes than others because they are born to rich parents and have advantages from the start	68
... there can never be equal opportunities in a society where some people have higher incomes than others	62
... people in Britain today have similar opportunities regardless of their income	27
Base	1,925

Source: National Centre for Social Research (2009)

importance of the higher earnings achieved by graduates, and the need to create a market in higher education where fees would vary according to teaching quality and students' purely economic prospects.

Finally, we review some more general attitudes to equal opportunities and equal outcomes. Table 6.4 shows that the British public generally agree that children from better-off families have many more opportunities than children from less well-off families: they clearly do not think that the education system enables children from poorer backgrounds to compete on even terms with others. And, in fact, 62 per cent of the public believe that equal opportunities and equal outcomes cannot be separated. They agree that there can never be equal opportunities in a society where some people have higher incomes than others.

The coalition government: social rights, policy reforms and welfare

T.H. Marshall (1992 [1950]) tracked the development of 'social rights' in the twentieth century, to follow the previous securing of civil rights (e.g. freedom of speech) and political rights (the right to vote) in the preceding two centuries. Social rights he took to imply the 'subordination of market price to social justice'. At a time of narrowing pay differentials, and increasing progressivity of income taxes, he was also able to declare that 'Class abatement is still the aim of social rights'. These social rights we may link directly to the creation of a new welfare state, and the tackling of Beveridge's five giant evils as part of post-war reconstruction – including that of ignorance, to be challenged by education.[4]

Social rights involve state funding, or at least the redistribution of resources from that which would occur under a free-market regime. They seek to promote equality, often in the face of stark inequality – inequality that we argue, below, is growing. Social rights will therefore always face challenges from those seeking to defend capital and the free market. Marshall wrote at a time of general optimism in a Keynes–Beveridge economic settlement. More recently, Esping-Andersen (1990) identified two key means by which capitalism may conflict with widening state welfare, which are highly relevant to this discussion. The first is a focus on the role of private market-based work ('commodification') and the potential materialism to which it gives rise, the second is the existence of strong hierarchies that perpetuate inequality and resist moves to greater equality. The 1980s saw increasing commodification and inequality but while the 'New Right' at that time may have aspired to make considerable reductions in welfare spending, and to roll back the frontiers of the state, they actually did relatively little, in practice, to change the basic parameters of the welfare state. The coalition government from 2010 onwards looks set to achieve the ambitions that proved beyond the New Right in the 1980s. We can see this in Figure 6.4, which shows that public spending (as a percentage of GDP) is forecast to drop in the UK to such an extent that it will be lower even than the prime neo-liberal country, the United States, by 2015 (Taylor-Gooby 2011).

The neo-liberal policies currently being adopted in higher education signal a sharp departure from the goals of social rights, and constitute a divergence found elsewhere within public policy reform. The coalition government is, in various areas of public policy, removing the role of state funding and thereby attempting to change the conception of what are thought of as state bodies, or those areas appropriate for state funding. Instead, the model is one of a fee-based approach, removing the notion of that service being provided either free or with subsidy. There are also clear reductions in the power of ordinary people to challenge powerful vested interests, and various moves to protect the wealth of those who are already well off. We look at a number of examples of such policies – affecting savings, legal aid and child maintenance. We then consider some wider changes that have been made to the system of social security benefits and tax credits.

One of the first acts of the coalition government was to abandon the planned introduction of the Saving Gateway, a special savings account for those on lower incomes (under £16,000 household income) providing a high rate of return on savings after two years. This was designed to help lower income groups develop a savings habit, and had been piloted in two different large-scale, testing evaluations. The 2010 emergency budget (HM Treasury 2010a) abolished the nascent Saving Gateway, on the grounds of its cost (this saved around £115 million); at the same time, measures were announced that increased the amounts that could be saved into ISAs (Individual Savings Accounts) – a tax-free method of saving and investing disproportionately benefiting the better-off, and that has never been subject to any kind of rigorous evaluation.

The Ministry of Justice is consulting on measures to reform legal aid, and in particular to reduce its overall cost. Assuming the proposals are enacted, legal aid would no longer be available for help with divorce costs nor with making claims for medical negligence. In both cases the power of those with large existing resources will be enhanced relative to those with limited resources on which to draw. Marshall specifically identified legal aid as part of the development of civil rights and social rights, noting that the legal system 'must not take a form which deprives the litigant of his right to justice or puts him at a disadvantage vis-à-vis his opponent' (1992 [1950]: 29) – whilst acknowledging the difficulties of reconciling equality with the prevalence of the market. The proposed changes to legal aid, unavailable to those making large medical claims against large private companies, or seeking to review benefits decisions made the state, certainly alter the balance of power between citizens and those they might be seeking to challenge.

Funding from legal aid goes, not just to lawyers, but also to independent advice such as that provided by the Citizens Advice Bureaux around the country. These CABs are often the first source of advice and support on legal and other issues. From April 2011, these organizations are also losing around £30 million in support from the Financial Inclusion Fund, likely to mean the loss of around 500 trained debt advisers. As the economy seeks to recover from a financially led crisis, and with unemployment remaining high, there will be fewer sources from which to seek assistance with indebtedness or with a variety of legal problems.

In the realm of child maintenance, separating parents are expected to

Figure 6.4 Public spending trends as per cent of GDP (2008–15)
Source: IMF 2010

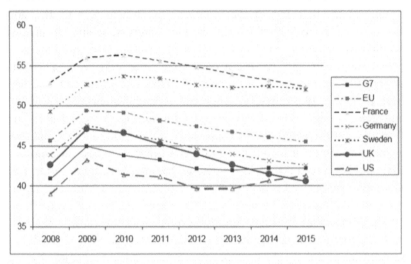

come up with their own arrangements, and will likely be penalized by charges and commission fees for the agency if they do not. Previously the Child Support Agency and the Children Maintenance and Enforcement Commission were expected to set and to collect child maintenance. Whilst it is well-known that these agencies did not always perform well in collecting what was due, the arrangements ensured that a third party was able to intervene between separating parents and at least attempt to deliver the outcomes that had been legislated for. In future parents will be expected to conduct more of the negotiations themselves, with the threat of additional charges and costs if they should seek to have these state agencies intervene on their behalf.

The effect of the January and April 2011 reforms is to reduce household incomes by around 3 per cent overall. The largest losses (as a proportion of income) will be at both the top and bottom of the income distribution. Middle-income families without children fare best from the reforms (Browne 2011). Working families with children are disproportionately affected (mostly by changes to the system of tax credits).

While it seems that those at the top will lose more than those in the middle, their levels of income and wealth (which increased dramatically in the 1980s as we saw above) are such that they could afford to contribute even more at a time of major cuts in public services and benefits. The coalition government has talked tough in relation to bank bonuses, non-domiciles and tax avoidance but has done very little, in practice, to crack down on these (Rowlingson 2011). But the Comprehensive Spending Review had relatively little to say about wealth and the wealthy. For example, in relation to reducing tax avoidance in the banking sector, the 2010 Spending Review stated that: 'The Government will continue to monitor tax receipts from the banking sector. As part of this, the Government expects the banking sector to comply with both the letter and the spirit of the law and not to engage in or promote tax avoidance' (HM Treasury 2010b: 30). This is a very softly-softly approach, particularly when compared with the government's hardline policies towards those on benefit, where people who do not take up job offers could lose their benefits for up to three years.

While wealth at the top is being protected, the incomes of those at the very bottom are under attack. Indeed, the largest single change to the system of benefits and tax credits is to change the basis of their uprating, from the Retail Prices Index (RPI) to the (generally lower) Consumer Prices Index (CPI). This switch from RPI-based uprating to CPI uprating will, over time, ensure that levels of taxes and benefits will be set on a lower path of growth and are likely to lag behind increases in earnings. To take one example, the level of Income Support for a family with two young children increased from £122 in April 1997 to reach £230 in 2009. Had benefits only been uprated by the CPI, they would have reached only £150. This switch of uprating approach will save the government around £6 billion in 2014–15 – which would have been greater, had not pensioners been largely spared this change. The older age group have received rather better treatment, with a 'triple lock' guaranteeing relatively favourable increases to the state retirement pension and increases to Pension Credit for those on lower incomes. Such a change is actually rather larger than the £3 billion being saved from the resource budget for higher education by 2014–15.

To the total saved may be added cuts of around £3 billion in tax credits for (mostly) working families, and £2 billion removed from the total budget for Housing Benefit. Whilst the government rhetoric has focused on the cuts in housing support to private tenants paying high rents in a few exceptional circumstances, much of the money saved is taken from social tenants through new restrictions on dwelling size and an expectation of greater rental contributions from family members. It is also proposed, in the longer term, that social tenants are treated more like private tenants in terms of the rents they pay and the degree of security of tenure they receive.

A clear emerging theme in the reforms is a suspicion of universalism and a focus on restricting support lower down the income distribution. This is seen in diverse policy reforms, including the removal of the tax credits for higher earners, plans to remove Child Benefit from higher rate taxpayers and the ending of the Child Trust Fund. There remains a heavily individualized account of the root causes of poverty – but it would be hard to argue that this is very different from the views of the preceding government.

Conclusions

Charles Tilly (1998) argued that groups with power try to retain the best opportunities for themselves, in what he called 'opportunity-hoarding'. In several respects we can see a new vision of marketized higher education that serves to maintain those with higher occupational status, and to diminish the opportunities for lower income groups to challenge those positions. We have already seen increases in inequality of incomes, as the highest earners race away from the middle earners. Some aspects of New Labour policy did try, temporarily and without great enthusiasm, to maintain and improve the incomes of those at the bottom of the income distribution. Nevertheless, they did not attempt to challenge the forces moving the UK towards higher levels of inequality. And the limited level of support towards lower income groups is most unlikely to be continued under the current government.

Having a degree may not be a guarantee of success, but over time graduates are able to open up a significant pay gap over those with lower qualifications. Those likely to benefit from this will need to understand something about how professional careers operate, and may need to postpone the receipt of rewards some time into the future. Both are traits we might recognize in those from professional family backgrounds, where parents can provide the necessary social, cultural, human and, crucially, economic capital to support their children through higher education.

Without a more level playing field earlier on in life, it will be extremely difficult for children from poorer backgrounds to access higher education. Too many young people currently leave school at sixteen, barely considering A levels, let alone higher education. This situation can be changed if we reduce inequality, support schools and further education colleges in disadvantaged areas and restore the Educational Maintenance Allowance. Greater regulation of universities' widening access policies would also help. And public resources for higher education could then also be justified and afforded if the wealthy were asked to contribute a fairer share towards the public finances.

Acknowledgements

Data from the British Social Attitudes Survey series were supplied by the UK Data Archive, and collected by the National Centre for Social Research in 2010. Data from the Labour Force Survey were also supplied by the UK Data Archive, and were collected by the Office for National Statistics and the Northern Ireland Statistics and Research Agency in 2010.

None of these organizations bears any responsibility for the analyses and interpretations reported on here. Any errors are the responsibility of the authors.

7

Universities and the Reproduction of Inequality

Diane Reay

Introduction

When the Browne Report was published I was re-reading R.H. Tawney who in the 1930s was advocating an educational system 'unimpeded by the vulgar irrelevancies of class and income' (Tawney 1943: 117). A key part of his social democratic vision was a universal university education, which he justified on the basis that university education was just as important for those who remain working class all their lives as it was for the upper and middle classes (Tawney 1964a). Rather, a socially just educational system was one in which education is seen as an end in itself, a space that 'people seek out not in order that they may become something else but because they are what they are' (1964a: 78), rather than a means of getting ahead of others or of stealing a competitive edge.

There was none of the crude instrumentalizing of education, including university education, that is endemic today. Instead, Tawney put the case for a common school asserting that 'the English educational system will never be one worthy of a civilised society until the children of all classes in the nation attend the same schools' (1964a: 144), and, I would add, until they attend the same universities.

These were the words of a public school boy who went to Oxford, but then had the good fortune to mix with and learn from ordinary men and women when he became a Workers Educational Association tutor in the 1910s. It appears that the government of 2011, with eighteen public schoolboys among its ministers and a substantial majority who are Oxbridge educated, has not benefited from Tawney's experience of social mixing. And there is a great deal of evidence that the elite universities still provide very little opportunity for social mixing across divisions of class or race. Indeed, Will Hutton (2007) compares the middle- and upper-class monopoly of Oxbridge with the closed shop practices of the old print unions and dock workers. Key to this class monopoly is the private school system.

Over the early 2000s, the Sutton Trust found that a third of all admissions to Oxbridge came from 100 schools (3 per cent of the total), 78 of which were private (2008b). In particular, Eton, St Paul's, Westminster and Winchester did massively better than their actual exam results would predict (Hutton 2007). In contrast, more recent research (Sutton Trust 2010a) found that less than 1 per cent of state school students on free school meals gain a place. As a result, students from private schools are fifty-five times more likely to get a place at Oxbridge than state educated free school meal pupils (Vasager 2010a).

This high degree of selectivity is not just limited to Oxbridge, the Sutton Trust found that the thirteen universities that ranked the highest in an average of published university league tables had an equally narrow school intake. Of the 100 schools with the highest intake to these elite universities, eighty-three were private, sixteen were grammar schools and only one was a comprehensive. As Michael Gove, the Education Secretary, told the Conservative Party conference in 2010, more students attending Westminster gain places at elite universities than the entire cohort of young people on free school meals (Gove 2010).

This is an issue not only of social class, but of race and ethnicity too. Official data shows that over twenty Oxbridge colleges made no offer to black students in 2009 and that one Oxford college had not admitted a black student in five years (Vasager 2010b). David Lammy (2010) found that, in 2009, 292 black students achieved three A grades at A level and that 475 black students applied to Oxbridge. However, only a handful were admitted, including just one British black Caribbean student to Oxford. In contrast, recent research suggests that white privately educated students are being over-selected relative to their exam results. Power and Whitty (2008) found that students from the private schools got into Oxbridge with lower point scores than their state educated peers. The mean A-level point score total for the Oxbridge graduates from state schools in their study was thirty-five, while the comparable figure for the privately educated students was thirty-one. One privately educated student even managed to gain a place with only fourteen A-level points.

The consequences of privileging an elite, segregated, private school system is that we have an educational system that is unfit for purpose in a globalized multicultural twenty-first century. Public schools are antiquated and dated institutions. Over seventy years ago, Tawney wrote of them that they were 'things of yesterday'. Their period of innovation was between the 1830s and the 1890s, since then they have simply consolidated and strengthened their primary function of reproducing our political and business elites. The private school system is impoverished by a vision that has no part to play in the twenty-first century, operating on the ethic, if it can be called such, of 'to each according to his/her income and property'. The private schools tie the UK to a model of society in which life chances are determined by birth and wealth, and competition and individualism are valorized. It is here we find the original seedbed of neo-liberal individualism, but a neo-liberalism further degraded by snobbery, elitism and intellectual superiority.

In 1909, Norwood and Hope described the public schools as producing: 'A race of well-bodied, well-mannered, well-meaning boys, keen at games, devoted to their schools, ignorant of life, contemptuous of all outside the pale of their own caste' (1909: 187). Today, we have the Oxbridge 'chav' parties and the private school student Facebook groups that talk about 'comprehensive school scum'. Both then and now there is ample evidence of the inability of many of the privately educated to mix on easy terms with any but small cliques. In the rest of this chapter I examine the underlying principles governing the Browne Report on fair access to higher education (and the government policies derived from it) before drawing on a range of voices both from my own research (Reay, David and Ball 2005; Reay, Crozier and James 2011) and the work of others to illustrate the consequences of the elitist educational policies we have inherited, and the ways in which they will be both sedimented and extended by the current reforms. I also consider the repercussions for the future of higher education.

The Browne Report: a triumph of money over mind

It is only through an understanding of insularity, class contempt and the sense of being more deserving that we can comprehend the recent Browne Report, an exemplar of the prioritizing of private gain over public good. Lord Browne, the first author of the report, is the former

Chief Executive of BP, and was educated at the King's School and St John's College, Cambridge. Four of his six fellow panel members were also educated at Oxbridge. Together they have produced a document driven by economic imperatives – these are evident in the language of sustainability and investment. In the first paragraph a link is made between economic growth and a strong higher education sector, while a little later the report asserts that higher education matters because a) it drives innovation and economic transformation and b) it helps produce economic growth. Any wider vision beyond a narrow economic instrumentalism is difficult to find. Instead we are told: 'Higher education is a major part of the economy, larger in size than the advertising industry and considerably larger than the aerospace and pharmaceutical industries. With an income of £23.4 billion a year it has been estimated as generating £59 billion of output' (Browne Report 2010: 15).

Vision is only mentioned once and then in the restricted sense of not being about shoring up the present system but enabling the widest number of students to benefit from the pleasures and opportunities of learning (Browne Report 2010: 58). In contrast, the term economic is used thirteen times. The assumption is that what students want to get from participating in higher education is money (Fish 2010). Tawney could have been writing of Lord Browne and his report when he asserted that: 'One of the besetting sins of those in high places in England is the bad utilitarianism which thinks that the object of education is not education but some external result, such as professional success or business leadership' (1964a: 85).

The focus of the Browne Report is on higher education as a source of private profit rather than public good. How far we have moved through a process of the instrumentalizing of higher education is visible in the text as we glimpse the extent to which it is increasingly dictated by the views, attitudes and values of business. This instrumentalizing of higher education gathered momentum under New Labour with the movement of responsibility for higher education from the Department for Education to the Department for Business and Enterprise, but it has accelerated under the current Liberal–Conservative coalition government. As Simon Head (2011) cogently argues, scholarship in British universities is increasing under threat from theories and practices conceived in American business schools and management consulting firms.

The main corollary of positioning higher education as a private investment is that there is no notion, in either the report or the government response to it, of higher education as a public good. If we adhere to notions of academic freedom and the public university, as I do, then there clearly is a need for reform to change practices introduced by the previous government. However, I would argue that this would look little like the reforms being enacted by the coalition government.

The university league: from premier to third division

The Browne Report asserts that higher education has become more diverse. It overlooks the fact that with diversity has come a three-tier system with the elite universities at the top and Oxbridge at their pinnacle, the red bricks in the middle with the 'post-1992' universities (the old polytechnics) at the bottom. While the latter group is diverse both ethnically and in socioeconomic terms, the elite universities are only slightly more diverse than they were forty years ago (*Guardian* 2010a). Although the Browne Report references HEFCE research that shows that in the last five years there has been a significant and sustained increase in the participation rate of young people living in the most deprived areas, what it does not highlight is the very low percentage of these young people who attend the elite universities (for example, only 2.7 per cent in Oxford and 3.7 per cent in Cambridge) (*Guardian* 2010b).

Peter Wilby (2010) is right in asserting that the introduction of student fees has been associated with a sharp rise in university participation. The statistics show that in 2009, young people from disadvantaged neighbourhoods were 50 per cent more likely to get university places than they had been fifteen years earlier, while those from advantaged areas were only 15 per cent more likely. However, what he fails to consider is exactly where those students go, and it is not to the elite universities. On the surface we appear to have a more inclusive higher education system, but the overall figures mask deep-seated divisions within that system, which are likely to be reinforced by the further increases in fees being proposed and by their differentiated character across universities.

The 2000s may have been the success story in widening access to university for working-class white and ethnic minority students, but that access has overwhelmingly been to the new universities. And just as many comprehensive schools were demonized as 'bog-standard' for having large cohorts of working-class students, so have the new universities. Rather, the 'massification' of the higher education sector

(Trow 2006; Guri-Rosenbilt *et al* 2007) has resulted in the reproduction of the UK school system's highly polarized and segregated hierarchy, with those new universities with sizeable cohorts of working-class students languishing at the bottom of the university league tables, while the Russell Group universities, with equally sizeable numbers of privately educated students, are at the pinnacle.

The problem of the private schools

Elitist attitudes to higher education run deep within British middle-class culture. Even those who defend the comprehensive principle in relation to schooling rarely seem to question the assumption that universities should be organized according to a rigid hierarchy. As Wilby recognizes, despite the laudable expansion of higher education over the last thirty years, entry to elite universities, 'those that all but guarantee entry to sought-after careers, still carries the heaviest social bias' (Wilby 2010). The result is a pernicious form of class apartheid that still exists despite the 'massification' of higher education (Trow 2006; Guri-Rosenbilt *et al* 2007).

The overwhelming focus on the educational failings of those at the bottom has meant that the issue of upper-class elitism and social closure has been relatively neglected. Yet, if we focus on the upper classes their relationship to education has barely changed since the seventeenth century – it still remains a means of retaining social status. Education for the upper classes is an essential and necessary imposition, and the main mechanism of upper-class cultural reproduction is private schooling, notwithstanding David Cameron's regular references to his children's state schooling. The English upper classes go through a very different transition from being a child to becoming an adult to that normative among either the middle or the working classes, in which private schools are central to socialization. For the upper classes it is culturally normative, particularly for males, to be sent away from home to a rigidly disciplined, often harsh, schooling. In doing so, notions of a happy childhood in the bosom of the family are relinquished for the certainty of social reproduction. Roald Dahl described his own experience of public schooling in the 1930s as: 'days of horrors, of fierce discipline, of not talking in the dormitories, no running in the corridors, no untidiness of any sort, no this or that or the other, just rules, rules and still more rules that had to be obeyed. And the fear of the dreaded cane hung over us like the fear of death all the time' (2001: 93).

When I interviewed one former public schoolboy, James, about his own experience 50 years earlier, there were still echoes of Dahl's dread, but also a vivid account of male upper class socialization. He said:

> At seven I got sent away to a prep boarding school... that was bad enough, the sense of being exiled. I missed my family, my mother in particular, terribly. But you know that was just what families like ours did and it was bruising in every way but at the same time there was a strange seductiveness about it. So I was at the receiving end of some serious bullying which just got worse as I got older so that by the time I was half way through I think I'd become brutalised by it all. I'd taken on the ethos, absorbed it to such an extent I began to think it was normal. I suppose that wasn't surprising because alongside the brutality there was friendship, support, a whole lot of nurture. You bought into the package and to an extent just got on with it but in retrospect a lot of it was horrific, as I said brutal and brutalising. But there was another aspect I still find deeply troubling when I looked back that we all just took for granted, this was how things were, you just got on with it.

What is muted in both these quotes is the elitism that lies at the heart of private schooling in the UK. This is captured starkly in the words of Will, a contemporary public school boy, who told me: 'We know we are the great and the good, that's obvious, what's less clear is which of us are going to be the leaders among the front runners.'

In 1931, when Tawney was writing *Equality*, he described how 'former public school boys filled cabinets, governed the empire, commanded in armies and navies, dominated boardrooms, crowded the judicial bench and were the mandarins of the civil service' (1964b: 76). Today, the situation remains almost exactly the same. In 2010 George Monbiot wrote: 'Through networking, confidence, unpaid internships, and most importantly attendance at top universities, the privately educated upper middle classes run politics, the civil service, the arts, the city, law, medicine, big business, the armed forces, even, in many cases, the protest movements challenging these powers' (2010).

The majority of those at the top of the leading professions, Will's 'front runners', are still educated in private schools that remain largely closed to the majority of the population. According to a recent Sutton Trust Report (2009) this includes seven in ten of the leading judges and barristers, as well as a majority of the partners at top law firms, leading journalists and medical practitioners. But it is the historic intertwining of the private schools with the elite universities that has been particularly pernicious.

Along with private education, access to Oxbridge is still the main educational route to the top professions. As Carole Cadwalladr points out, Oxbridge is 'a short hop, skip and a jump into the heart of the British establishment' (Cadwalladr 2008). Eight in ten barristers and judges studied at either Oxford or Cambridge, as did a majority of top solicitors; 62 per cent of ministers in the current coalition government went to private schools and 69 per cent were educated at Oxbridge (Sutton Trust 2010b). The relational significance of all this is brought powerfully to life in the following statistics: in 2009, 79 male students receiving free school meals in state schools achieved three As at A level; in the same year 175 young men at Eton achieved three As; the number of children in 2009 who were eligible for free school meals, bearing in mind that every year 600,000 children attend state schools, was 80,000, of whom just 45 made it to Oxbridge.

Currently the 'short hop' from the private schools to Oxbridge and then into the upper echelons of the professions is perpetuating an insular, inward-looking, ruling elite. The seamlessness of upper middle-class social reproduction is evident in the quotes below:

Deciding which university was probably a very unscientific process actually. My father went to Trinity in Cambridge to do law and he was always very keen to show her his own college which he did when she was about thirteen and she fell in love with it.
(Mother of privately educated student)

Well just since I've been born, I suppose it's just been assumed I am going to university because both my parents went to university, all their brothers and sisters went to university and my sister went to university so I don't think I've even stopped to think about it ... I've just grown up with the idea that's what people do. I have always assumed I am going to university.
(Nick, private school student)

Nick went on to point out that all these members of his family had been to either Oxford or Cambridge. The words in both quotes evoke images of elite conveyor belts rather than considered rational choice – it is just what 'people like us do'. As myself and colleagues wrote at the time, 'this is a non-decision', almost too obvious to articulate (Reay *et al.* 2005). Rather choice was automatic, taken-for-granted and always assumed. Financial concerns and worries were never raised. These families belong to the section of society who will be paying substantially less for an elite university education, even at the level of fees currently proposed, than they paid for their children's schooling.

Disrupting notions of 'the best'

While the current structure of higher education needs to be extensively criticized there is also a need for a more philosophic discussion about what 'the best' constitutes in the higher education context. In particular, it is important to question the association of the elite universities with what is best in higher education. As the students I interviewed demonstrated, the homogeneity found in the elite universities can be both intellectually stifling and socially limiting. In my research with Gill Crozier and John Clayton (Reay *et al* 2009) we looked at working-class students who went to elite universities. Their narratives reveal the intellectual stimulation and growth that comes with attending places like Oxford and Cambridge. At the same time their accounts are an interesting counterbalance to conventional academic hierarchies that position universities like the one they attended as 'the best'. While on one level they recognize and are grateful for the 'value-added' they are gaining academically, and are fiercely loyal about their university, the students all have a reflexive critique of the costs and losses, as well as the gains, in attending such universities. And these critiques all hinge one way or another on homogeneity. For all the students, there is too much sameness and not enough difference at elite universities.

We found that, even among those students who do successfully make the transition from working-class home to elite higher education institution, many of the same feelings and attitudes led the majority of high achieving working-class students to reject places like Oxford and Cambridge. For all the students in the elite university we referred to as 'Southern', it represented neither normativity, nor balance. Like the working-class students in Bufton's (2002) study, they made a distinction between 'the real world' and the academic world. They presented a university world of over-performativity, arcane practices and slightly autistic behaviour. This is evident in what Nicole says:

Like this notion of time is so intense, we refer to it as the Southern bubble because the nicest experience you can get when you're at Southern is leaving it ... As soon as I realize I'm out of the city it's like a huge weight just goes and I'm like there's a real world out there. People will wake up the next morning if their essay isn't finished. People will still have a heart beating if they haven't finished their reading. The world isn't ending if you haven't finished your work. That's what the Southern bubble is, it's a time warp, it's so weird, so regimented by deadlines. (Nicole)

There is no talk here about academic brilliance and being 'the brightest of the bright', but rather an ironic recognition of the compulsive obsessive workaholic dispositions that constitute the highly successful academic habitus. For the most part, these students have a critically reflexive, questioning stance on Southern and what it represents. Critiques range from Nicole's observations that Southern is far too rarefied and segregated from the real world to Jamie's passionate assertion that, 'Southern needs to pull in lots more non-traditional students but also to actively discourage private and selective state school students.' With such views it is perhaps unsurprising that four of the nine students we interviewed were actively engaged in outreach work with non-selective state schools, trying to encourage other non-traditional students to apply.

At the time our research was being conducted a national broadsheet published an article on the front page entitled 'Education apartheid as private schools flood elite universities' (Paton 2007). Academically successful working-class students gain enormously from studying at institutions like Southern, flourishing as learners and growing in confidence, both academically and socially. The gains to the university are far less likely to be considered. In a period when the chances of working-class students, like the ones in our study, attending Southern are set to fall dramatically, I would argue that the ability of universities like Southern to renew and revitalize themselves, to became fully 'paid-up' members of the global, multicultural twenty-first century, is crucially dependent on attracting the very students who are going to be excluded.

As Archer and Leathwood argue, the assumption is always that it is 'the working-class individual who must adapt and change, in order to fit into, and participate in, the (unchanged) higher education institutional culture' (2003: 176). A second irony then has been the failure of the widening access and participation debate to recognize elite universities need non-traditional students just as much as the students need them.

Both need the other in order to flourish, the students academically and the universities socially. Within the recent status quo, an enormous number of working-class students were excluded from realizing their academic potential and the coalition policy changes will exclude even greater numbers. Yet, equally worrying and even less recognized is the failure of the elite universities to realize their potential for combining academic excellence with a rich social diversity. Giddens (1991) has written about the dangers of an economically privileged and politically powerful elite floating free of connection with the vast majority of society. The elite universities risk becoming gated academic communities, white upper- and upper-middle-class ghettos: Nicole's privileged bubble, but with no way in and no way out.

The consequences of the privatization of higher education

Despite right-wing assertions that working-class young people will not be deterred by increased fees, existing research suggests otherwise. The Sutton Trust (2008a) found that aversion to debt was the major reason cited by young people for not going to university: 59 per cent of those who had decided not to pursue higher education reported that avoiding debt had affected their decision either 'much' or 'very much'. The government now plans to raise the basic threshold for tuition fees at English universities to £6,000 a year, with institutions allowed to charge up to £9,000 in 'exceptional circumstances', circumstances which have rapidly become normalized. Students currently pay £3,290 a year. Atherton *et al.* (2010) questioned 2,700 young people aged between eleven and sixteen in 2010 and found that among those who would have been likely to go to university, only 68 per cent would still be confident of this if fees went up to £5,000, while if they had to pay £7,000 only 45 per cent would still be keen. Raising the cost of a degree to £5,000 a year would deter almost half of those from the most deprived backgrounds who would otherwise have gone on to higher education, while raising fees to £7,000 would cut the number by nearly two-thirds. The result of these changes is that the UK now combines the lowest spending on higher education of any comparable OECD country with the highest tuition fees for study at a public university. When tuition fees were first introduced in 1998, the additional income was invested in universities. However, this government has proposed that the biggest spending cut of all should fall on higher education. It has raised tuition fees in order to achieve a massive public disinvestment in higher education (to be replaced by public investment in a loans system that will increase indebtedness and act as a disincentive to those from poorer families).

This massive disinvestment in higher education will further exacerbate the growing divide between those students with parents who are able to subsidize their living costs sufficiently to enable them actually to be students and the growing majority who do not. Under the new regime this latter group will grow exponentially. A study by the Higher Education Careers Services Unit (Hecsu) revealed in November 2010 that, even at current levels, student debt is leading more final-year students to take on part-time jobs during term-time and to work longer hours. But students at Oxford and Cambridge are not allowed to work in term-time and, indeed, the academic work expectations make it virtually impossible for them to do so. This will further deter working-class students from applying, especially as they are increasingly going to have to work throughout their university education in order to defray some of the mounting debts they are incurring.

While none of the privately educated students or their parents I interviewed mentioned financial worries, that was in sharp contrast to their working-class counterparts. When we conducted the research, students were expected to pay fees that were far lower than the new expectation of £6,000 to £9,000, yet working-class students talked constantly about the financial risks (Reay *et al* 2001). The head of sixth form of a predominantly working-class, multiethnic north London comprehensive told us:

> There is an awful lot of concern about whether I can possibly afford to do this, whether I can possibly afford to take the risk, to take out student loans and self-finance my education. There is a process of having to say although it's very bleak there's a light at the end of the tunnel. But already students are worrying, have a lot of anxiety about how will their families afford this.

However, it is not only my own research which demonstrates the barriers confronting both white and black working-class students considering the elite universities. Current research by Graeme Atherton and colleagues (2010) found that 79 per cent of the working-class young people they surveyed in London and Merseyside still wanted to go to university but that 42 per cent were not prepared to pay fees of more than £5,000, and that percentage rose for those on free school meals, only 20 per cent of whom were willing to pay more than £5,000. They also found pervasive reluctance to borrow the sums that will be required if they are to realize their aspirations to attend university. There was also little appetite for shorter courses or part-time study (less than 25 per cent). The study also looked at what the government's promise of £150 million in scholarships would mean in practice. If fees average £7,000, 6,944 students in receipt of free school meals will be able to have scholarships; if the fees rise to £9,000 the number would be 5,555. This contrasts sharply with the number of such young people, 10,570, who went to university in 2009.

Of even more concern than the survey results were the themes of anxiety and loss that emerged from the small qualitative research that accompanied it (O'Rourke *et al* 2010). The words 'worry' and 'worried' came up 182 times in 6 focus group interviews, accompanied by a strong sense of loss. The young people and their parents talked about the loss and the threat of losing potentially good teachers, doctors and social workers, and what this means in terms of the loss to wider society if working-class young people were not able to study the courses at university they aspired to. They made the important point that just because some young people and their families can afford a course in medicine it does not mean that they are the right people for the job. Rather, the right person and their contribution to society may be lost because they can no longer afford to do such a course.

The onslaught of privatization within the university sector is not just about turning a university education from a public entitlement into a private investment most working-class young people cannot afford, it is also an attack on the university as a public institution. There has been a creeping privatization of higher education over the last twenty years, resulting in over 25 per cent of universities outsourcing aspects of their work from the running of their student residences to the maintenance of their buildings. However, now right-wing think-tanks such as Policy Exchange are strongly advocating more far-reaching privatization of many university services (Shepherd 2010). The stated objective, 'greater efficiency' is yet another spurious means to open up the university sector to what is termed 'the free market'. However, the main consequence is the transformation of a public institution into a source of profit for many private firms.

Conclusion

Terry Eagleton argues that we have seen the death of universities as centres of critique. Rather, the role of academia has become one of 'servicing the status quo, not challenging it in the name of justice, tradition, imagination, human welfare, the free play of the mind or alternative visions of the future' (2010). The Browne Report is another nail in the coffin of the public university and a critical questioning academia. Its neo-liberal economizing is part of a wider right-wing drive to reshape education as just another market commodity (Lynch 2006). It is also yet another barrier to social mobility. Social mobility has become the chimera of modern times, continuously talked about, endlessly exaggerated, but more myth than reality.

In the late 1960s I went to university despite discouragement from teachers and personal lack of knowledge and information about higher education. I went because, as long as working-class young people succeeded educationally, higher education was a free right and entitlement open to them just as much as to their richer peers. I would not be going now, and I certainly would not be going once the new funding regime is implemented. The welfare state gave fresh hope and optimism to families like my own. Our forbears had been in service, worked down the mines and died in the workhouses, but developing forms of universal public provision bestowed a new sense of worth, entitlement and value, and the prospect of a better, brighter future. The contemporary political message is very different. Clever working-class children are entitled to go to university, but only if they are prepared to accrue debts that may well total £50,000 (and, indeed, potentially much more). Government and the state are not prepared to invest in them as potential graduates. They are no longer worth the risks involved, which they must now bear themselves. What we will be left with, particularly in our elite universities, is the triumph of the logic that Tawney ironically labelled 'the beautiful English arrangement by which wealth protects learning, and learning in turn admits wealth as a kind of honorary member of its placid groves' (1964a: 81). The vast majority of young people from poorer background will be relegated to what are perceived to be second and third division universities, encumbered with debts they have little prospect of ever paying off. A great deal of rhetoric about social mobility and equalities has emanated from the Liberal–Conservative coalition government but its higher education policies reveal that not only does the emperor have no clothes, he is rapidly dying of hypothermia.

Afterword: A Positive Future for Higher Education in England

Professor Sir Steve Smith

I disagree with other contributors to this book. My core claim is that the future is indeed positive, not in some Panglossian sense, but rather because many of the reforms carried out by the coalition government and its predecessor are aimed, at least in part, at strengthening the overall standing of HE with regards to its global competitors. That is decidedly not the common understanding, and I fully accept that my perspective will be controversial. But whatever my personal views of the proportion of the HE system that should be funded by the taxpayer (for the record, I support more of the cost of HE coming from the taxpayer than the system to be introduced in 2012 will require), I am clear that the recent changes will strengthen England's universities. I want to use this afterword to explain why I believe that to be the case. I will try and be as clear and explicit as possible, in order that my claims can either be proved or disproved by future events.

Over the past two years, as President of Universities UK (UUK), I have worked closely with both this government and the Labour administration during the most significant period of change in HE in this country since the 1960s. The result of their decisions mean that universities face some momentous financial as well as cultural challenges that will affect profoundly everything that they do. Much of the change we are experiencing has been driven by the fiscal environment, but there is also a strong push to introduce wider changes such as more competition, a more responsive student-centred system, greater transparency, and a focus on efficiency and value for money. The changed funding arrangements will create a very different HE environment, and it likely that we will also end up with a new regulatory landscape.

And the sector faces a significant PR task in communicating to the general public what the changes really mean for the students of the future. But I believe that the future for HE is not bleak and will not mean that students from less well-off backgrounds will be disadvantaged. I believe in the long term that students will get a better experience of HE and better value for money as a result of them.

Changes introduced by the Labour government

It is worth noting at the outset that the cutbacks in funding for English HE did not start with the arrival of the new coalition government: the Labour government had already announced plans for significant cutbacks in HEFCE funding, and had set up Lord Browne's review and agreed its terms of reference with the Conservative Party. The aim of the review was to deal with the unsustainable costs of the student loans system, the underestimating of which had led to consequent reductions in funding for universities of about £449 million by 2010–11, with a further £600 million reduction to come by 2013. To that £1,049 million cut was to be added HE's share of the planned 12 per cent cut across government spending proposed by the Labour government in advance of the 2010 election. That 12 per cent would have equated to an additional £1.6 billion. So, just to be completely clear, the choice was never between a coalition government that cut HE and a Labour government that would not have cut HE. In truth, the coalition government has cut HE by more than Labour would have done, but not by so much more as might be thought. My calculations suggest a coalition government cut to the university/science/student support budgets of about £3 billion in addition to the Labour government's imposed cuts of £449 million, compared to a Labour government's projected cut of about £1.6 billion in addition to the £449 million.

A new government

But of course, it became immediately clear to UUK that the new coalition government started from a very clear commitment to reducing government spending. I warned of the consequences of such reductions in a series of newspaper articles (Lambert and Smith 2009; Smith 2010a; Smith 2010b; Smith 2010c). But clearly UUK needed to be pragmatic and try to maximize the amount of funding that came to universities. Indeed, that was the position the UUK Board consistently took. The obvious problem was that if we were unable to persuade the new government that HE should not be cut significantly, then we would have to find the money from other sources. Obviously, we did not succeed in persuading the new government that there should be no cuts to HE, but it is critically important to note that the outcome of all the changes to the funding regime is that universities in England will get about 10 per cent more cash in 2014 than in 2010. That is not a real-terms increase, of course, but it is a far better outcome than those of the vast majority of the publicly funded sectors. Nor, I readily admit, will the funding be distributed in the same way as it is currently. There will be winners and losers, but these winners and losers are not simply distributed on an old hierarchy, but from all we know about the cost bases of different types of institutions (and we have excellent data on costs) it is clear that there will be winners and losers across all the four main mission groups in the sector.

This decision to minimize the reductions in funding to universities meant that we based our case on the economic role of universities. We faced such a strong call for significant reductions in direct public funding to universities that we felt the language of economics was the only language that would secure the future prosperity of our universities and higher education institutions. This language generated a sense amongst many that long-cherished ideals about the educational and social purposes of higher education were under threat, and perhaps disappearing forever. But the political reality was that the severity of the difficulties facing the government in dealing with the public finances meant a reduction in public financing was completely inevitable. Indeed, by late June 2010 we had a clear indication of the likely level of such reductions, and we spent the summer of 2010 fighting to limit those cutbacks.

Our core argument was that HE played not only a major educational and social role, but also a massive economic role. HE was, we claimed, a great success story and it would be madness to damage it. This is because universities are critical agents of economic regeneration and growth, as well as creators of knowledge. Research-intensive universities have a key role to play in generating curiosity-driven research and knowledge transfer. They attract around them high-quality businesses, and also help develop societies that can thrive in a globalized, competitive economy: a society where skills, knowledge and industry are important. According to a report published by the National Endowment for Science, Technology and the Arts (NESTA) in 2010, new knowledge and innovation has generated at least two-thirds of productivity growth in the UK over the past ten years (Shanmugalingam *et al* 2010). The UK sells more brainpower per capita than anywhere else in the world. In 2005, this amounted to £75 billion in knowledge services – a quarter of all UK exports.

And the industries at the heart of the knowledge economy are dependent on universities for the creation of an educated and highly skilled workforce. Universities are the engine rooms of the modern global economy. Our universities pump about £59 billion into the economy each year. That's 2.3 per cent of the annual Gross Domestic Product of the UK – a bigger direct contribution to the economy than the advertising and pharmaceutical industries. And I am proud to say that in the UK we have one of the very best quality university systems in the world.

The arguments for knowledge

I would like to state unequivocally that UUK strongly opposed the massive reductions in public spending on higher education. However, the utterly inevitable abandonment of the state's direct role in funding universities meant that we had no choice but to focus our efforts on securing an alternative income stream for higher education – or risk losing forever our international reputation as one of the best HE systems in the world. As I have said, this was achieved by focusing our arguments on the economic role played by universities, and particularly research.

If you start with the future of the UK economy, as the coalition government claimed to do when it came to power, the logic was to ask what choices we had over the kind of economy the UK will be in the future, and then to ask what this implied for the research base. Higher level skills were also a key part of the story. Of course, similar arguments can be made about the role of universities in social mobility, social justice and social inclusion, but in the case of the research base I argued that there is literally no substitute for the role that universities play if the UK was to secure a successful economy in the future. We tailored a narrative that did not start with the universities and what might be good for them, but with the economy, and specifically with the best strategy to ensure future economic growth. It was critically important for universities to emphasize to government the importance of not making decisions that would fundamentally undermine our future capacity to be a globally competitive knowledge economy. No other sector argued as strongly the criticality of its role in determining the nature of the future economy.

NESTA's Report (Shanmugalingam *et al.* 2010) argued this with incisive clarity. Looking at four scenarios for future economic growth (business-as-usual; manufacturing renaissance; high-tech flourishing; innovation across the economy), it concluded that the best chances for future economic growth come from the last two scenarios, and in each case they highlight 'the important role that ... the so called knowledge economy... [has] in driving growth over the next decade' (2010: 28).

Of course, we had been here before: the previous government commissioned two reports that looked at the skills needed for such a knowledge economy (Leitch 2006) and at government's science and innovation policies (Sainsbury Report 2007). Taken together these reports painted a detailed, evidence-based and compelling account of what kinds of skills and research the UK needed to compete in the future. Indeed, the central conclusion of the Leitch report (that the proportion of jobs requiring skills of level 4 or above will increase from 29 per cent to 40 per cent by 2020) has recently been reinforced by recent reports by both the CBI (Confederation of British Industry 2011) and the UKCES Skills Audit (UK Commission for Employment and Skills 2010); both argue for substantial increase in rate of participation in HE in order for the UK to remain globally competitive as a knowledge economy.

Lord Sainsbury's report, *The Race to the Top* (Sainsbury Report 2007), is the most intellectually convincing report on the topic that I have ever read. It is the alpha and omega of analysis on how science and research policy relate to economic growth. It presents a joined up analysis, has a clear vision and provides a long-term strategy for maximizing innovation and economic growth. Its core claim is that the UK cannot possibly win a race to the bottom on low wage rates for low added-value jobs, and thus has to win the race to the top by creating high value-added jobs. To do this requires investing in the innovation eco-system. He concludes that 'we can be a winner in "the race to the top", but only if we run fast' (Sainsbury Report 2007: 2).

Given that conclusion, the UK Trade and Investment's July 2010 report on inward investment, with a preface by William Hague and Vince Cable, makes interesting reading. It argued that currently the UK has the strongest research base in Europe. It stated: 'For international companies, the benefits of locating in the UK to access the world class R&D base remain clear – for example, overseas entities own 37% of patents in the UK, compared with just 11.2% in the USA and just 4.4% in Japan' (UK Trade and Investment 2010: 12). But it warned that 'the international competitive environment to win high value R&D investment is intense' with 80 per cent of the £400 billion annually invested by the 1,000 largest companies concentrated in just five countries (the United Kingdom, Germany, France, Japan and the United States).

Our international competitors are investing in their R&D bases. Here the UK compares poorly. Using the latest OECD figures, whereas the UK spends 1.78 per cent of GDP on R&D, Sweden spends 3.73 per cent, Japan 3.39 per cent, Korea 3.23 per cent, the United States 2.62 per cent and Germany 2.53 per cent (OECD 2010).

The data presented a depressing picture in terms of the comparison between UK investment decisions over science and research and those of our major competitors. For example, the United States doubled its science spend to 2016, with a $21 billion increase in science and research over the next two years alone. Germany announced an additional €18 billion for science and R&D from 2010–15, on top of current spend of €30 billion. China announced an additional $860 million research support fund. And France announced an additional €8 billion for research over five years, including €3.5 billion on world-class innovation clusters and €1 billion for the creation of research centres of excellence in universities, plus an additional €11 billion for HE generally. The only countries reducing their research funding at a time of global recession were Spain, the Czech Republic and Ecuador.

And all the international and UK evidence pointed to one inescapable conclusion: in R&D, it is governmental spending that leverages out private-sector spending. Government R&D spending is a magnet for private investment and, crucially, for inward investment. A reduction in governmental R&D spending thus starts a vicious circle, leading not to replacement private R&D spending but to reductions in private spend. Business leaders made their position clear in letters to *The Times* and to the *Daily Telegraph* on 16 June 2010, in which a group of CEOs wrote that: 'We need a credible plan for restoring fiscal balance but urge the government to be cautious over those elements of public spending that are vital to the future growth and prosperity of our economy – science, innovation and knowledge.'

At the time that negotiations over the Spending Review settlement were at its height, I used the analogy that cutting back on the UK's R&D base would the equivalent of the government cutting back on the production of Spitfires in the early summer of 1940. I wanted the government to be in no doubt about the risks these cuts in funding posed to the world-class standing of higher education in this country. Indeed, as I argued in the *Guardian* in October 2010, the day before the government's Spending Review, where exactly was the government's mandate for cutting spending on HE (Smith 2010c)? I also pointed out that: 'While many commentators see Browne as offering savings to the Treasury by introducing increased graduate contributions, it is the spending review that sets the context within which to understand Browne. Browne is not the cause of the reductions in state funding; it is an attempt to substitute other funding sources for lost government revenue.' I noted 'how strongly opposed UUK is to tomorrow's announcements of these massive reductions,' adding that the government 'should be in no doubt about the risks these cuts in funding pose to the world-class standing of our higher education system, and thus to the country's future economic growth and prosperity. The UK's competitors face the same deficit reduction challenges as we do, but they have decided to invest in higher education at this crucial time, not cut it.'

In reality, the government did not cut universities as much as UUK feared. A week before the Spending Review, we had been warned that the cut to the science (i.e. research council and quality-related [QR]) budget would be around 12–20 per cent. It turned out to be protected in cash (but not real) terms. Nonetheless, as expected, there remained a massive reduction in planned funding to universities: the expectation of this had led UUK the week before to welcome Lord Browne's proposals. We thought that they would achieve better outcomes (in terms of financial sustainability, promoting access, reducing low-earner repayments on student loans, enhancing student choice and improving the quality of the student experience) than would be possible without them. There were wider potential consequences that would transform higher education in the UK to be borne in mind, most obviously the replacement of the state as funder by the student/graduate, and the withdrawal of state funding from nearly all social science and humanities subjects. State funding becomes almost completely concentrated on student support. The creation of a real market in home undergraduate students, in terms of price and numbers, would rely on student choice to drive quality and efficiency, and will remove the predictability of the current state funding system at a stroke. This is an uncomfortable place to be for many of us in higher education. But it's happening. This new landscape is coming up on the horizon and there is no turning back.

Prevailing myths about the new higher education landscape

Although universities continue to be the focus of public attention, it is surprising how many myths and untruths prevail in the popular imagination about the new system. Undoubtedly, the issues we have been debating, and are still debating, are absolutely critical to future generations. They are central to how Britain sees itself in future decades, its position in the world economy, our ability to develop our citizens, how we adapt to long-term challenges such as environmental sustainability, a shifting balance of global power and the need to diversify our own economy.

As Alison Wolf (2011) pointed out in her review of vocational education, participation in higher education is now a near universal aspiration. Among mothers of children born in 2000, 98 per cent want their child to go to university. That is a radically different picture from when I was studying for a degree. Then around one in seven people went into higher education and less than 10 per cent of people from the lowest income brackets did so.

Because of this we must fully engage with, and indeed welcome, the debate. And we must be clear that quietly wishing nothing will change is simply not an option.

Let me focus on three key myths that have become established in the public debate. The first is that funding for higher education has been reduced. Second, that this spells the end for humanities and social sciences. And third, that the new system places impenetrable barriers in the way of students from poorer backgrounds.

Higher education funding

As I have already noted, I have argued throughout the debate that the government must not leave universities with a massive gap in funding. With HE and research making up the bulk of Department for Business, Innovation and Skills (BIS) spending, it was always going to be the case that direct funding to universities would face a sharp reduction. Yet there was no guarantee initially that government would be able to deliver replacement funding through a higher fee cap.

We now face a radical recasting of the funding model for HE. The BIS annual resource allocation for HE will fall by £2.9 billion by 2015. The direct HEFCE grant for teaching will reduce from around £5 billion to around £2 billion as new tuition fee income comes on stream. Research and science spending is frozen in cash terms. The capital budget is being cut by 44 per cent and we should not forget the knock-on effects of policy changes in health and teaching that will likely reduce university income further.

But government support for higher education is not ending. Instead, its direction is being shifted dramatically. As David Willetts pointed out at UUK's 2011 spring conference, the government expects to be spending around £6.5 billion in tuition loans, £3.5 billion in maintenance loans and £2 billion in maintenance grants and scholarships on top of the remaining teaching grant in 2014–15. The balance in funding between teaching grant and loans is currently about two-thirds to one-third. By 2014–15 the balance is expected to be around 80/20 loans to teaching grant. The fees announcements from across the sector could make this bill considerably higher.

That is a radical shift that is driven by a clear political aim: to introduce more market incentives into the system. Those market drivers mean that universities have to be clear about what we offer: that is, a high-quality product, provision of skills and experiences that will directly benefit the student, and adding real value to them as individuals as they go through life.

Crucially, based on an average annual tuition fee of £7,500, the sector will be getting 10 per cent *more income* than it does currently by 2014–15.

This is good news, although we must acknowledge that it comes with significant consequences and risks. There will be a risk of market failure for institutions, and the student as 'co-investor' will pose institutions with a distinct set of expectations to meet. These are very big questions that everyone working in higher education will need to consider. And it concerns me that HEFCE will not have the level of resources necessary to be able to intervene in case of market failure.

It is worth noting one other oddity about the financing of HE. Paradoxically, the outlay of government on HE is significantly greater from 2012 than it is currently. As I argued in the *Guardian* in March 2011, 'while funding to HEFCE reduces by about £3bn by 2014, public spending on fees and maintenance loans is expected to increase by about £4.3bn – and spending on student grants is also likely to increase by about £0.6bn. This equates to an increase of about £2bn in public spending on HE by 2014' (Smith 2011). As I have said, the reality is that the government will spend much more on HE in 2014 than it does in 2011. The explanation for this seeming paradox lies in the arcane rules of government accounting. Cash advanced to the Students Loan Company (SLC) to pay to universities on behalf of students does not count as public expenditure: the only part that counts is the estimated amount that will not be re-paid – the Resource Accounting and Budgeting (RAB) charge – which currently is estimated at 31 per cent. This is not classified as cash expenditure in the year in which the money is spent, but only as a charge to hit the national accounts when the unpaid debt is forgiven after thirty years. The savings to government therefore come from the fact that the reduction in HEFCE funding of about £3 billion is only offset during the year by the increased grant expenditure (of £600 million) and by the RAB charge of about £1.33 billion. Government thus spends about £2 billion more each year, but the national accounts record this as a net reduction of about £1.07 billion.

Humanities and social sciences

The second myth assumes that the Humanities and Social Sciences (HASS) subjects will be unable to compete in this new environment. On the one hand, the skills that HASS students acquire are relevant to the modern jobs market. UUK's (2011) report on the creative industries made that clear, for example. That means students will continue to be attracted to high-quality courses. David Willetts has spoken publicly about the importance of these subjects and has acknowledged that almost every big issue in society needs to be looked at from the perspective of different disciplines. Sir Adam Roberts (Roberts 2011), President of the British Academy, has also recently made a robust case for the sustainability of HASS subjects. He pointed out that the disciplines are thriving with a 40 per cent increase in student numbers between 2001–2 and 2009–10. International recruitment has been particularly strong and is no doubt driven in part by the world-class standard of research outputs. Sir Adam called for threats to be accurately identified and for solutions to be tailored to suit. And I am in no doubt that the key solution is a continued focus on quality and on equipping students with essential skills.

But the biggest concerns relate to the future levels of funding of the HASS subjects. Well, contrary to the myth, they have not been adversely hit by funding reductions. Indeed, we are now seeing a reaction from those in Science, Technology, Engineering and Mathematics (STEM) subjects who now realize that the new funding regime is more favourable to the HASS subjects.

This is for three main reasons: first, no subject has had its QR funding raided in cash terms. Second, every single subject studied in this country, even medicine, has had its government teaching funding cut by at least the same amount as has hit the HASS subjects (HEFCE Bands C and D disappear, and the same amount is taken from Bands A and B, but in addition Band B is reduced by about a further £600 per student). Third, and most significantly, the £9,000 maximum fee means that HASS subjects get significantly more funding than they currently receive. The basic calculation is that the current Bands D and C resources, including the student fee are (in 2010–11) about £5,950 and £7,125 gross, or after Office for Fair Access (OFFA) reductions, a net figure of about £5,450 and £6,625 respectively. Under the new fee regime, these figures become £9,000 gross and £8,100 net. That translates into an increase of about 48 per cent for Band D and 22 per cent for Band C. To be fully comparable, lost teaching capital needs to be subtracted from the new fee levels, which reduces the increases to about 41 per cent and 16 per cent respectively. Of course, not all institutions will charge £9,000, but then again they will pay significantly less of a payment to satisfy OFFA.[1]

These figures have led to a feeling amongst colleagues working in STEM-dominant institutions that HASS subjects will be able to spend much more on the student experience and on staff-student ratios than will be available for STEM subjects. This is because the residual HEFCE funding for Band B subjects only results in a total resource of £10,500, compared to a resource of £9,000 for Band C and Band D subjects. Overall funding thus increases much more for humanities and social science subjects than for STEM subjects. Of course, institutions may want or need to cross-subsidize STEM by top-slicing HASS subjects, but then again many would argue that this has always happened. However you look at it, though, HASS subjects are in a far better financial position after the reforms than before them. But, to repeat, this is not exactly the commonly accepted view of their fate.

Access and widening participation

But doesn't the new system of funding mean that we face a form of financial apartheid in access to higher education? Let me state absolutely clearly that I am committed to maintaining the widest possible participation in higher education and to expanding access in traditionally low take-up parts of the community. No one should be deterred from going to university by fear of the costs if they can benefit from the experience. Worst of all would be for anyone to be deterred by a misunderstanding about the costs.

The student financial support package has been deliberately designed to minimize the costs for those graduates who are least able to pay. There has been some concern about the future costs of the system but the government must maintain its commitment to fair access through its package of student support. Also, all higher education institutions have a responsibility to provide support for widening participation (WP). Those charging more than the basic fee level must prove that they can fulfil their obligations in this regard. Information, advice and guidance to students must also be right. Potential students must not be encouraged away from higher education because of misapprehensions among teachers and parents. That demands a real commitment of resources and willingness for all universities to work together across government and with schools.

However, the main issues concern the effect of the changes in university funding on access and social mobility. I have been involved with HE admissions for many years, both at institutional level and at a national level, including representing UUK on the UCAS Board, chairing the Higher Education strand of the National Council for Educational

Excellence under the last Labour government, and as a member of the Delivery Partnership which delivered a series of reforms to the current application process. I am also about to take up chairmanship of the Supporting Professionalism in Admissions Programme. I have always maintained vehemently that access to higher education has to be free at the point of delivery; access to students from low socioeconomic backgrounds has to be enhanced by a system of institutional bursaries and government grants; there has to be a system of student financing that deals with the distinct problems of part-time students; and the outcome has to preserve the essential link between the student and the institution they attend. Universities act as vehicles to facilitate upward social mobility and, by doing so, make a significant contribution to creating a society that is economically equitable and socially just. It is vitally important therefore, that we maintain a fair admissions system where suitably qualified people are able to access the programmes and institutions that best meet their needs and aspirations regardless of their background or social class, and that everyone understands this and has confidence in the integrity of the admissions process.

Sadly, we know that not all young people have an equal chance of attaining the highest grades of which they are capable. This is borne out in the research that Mark Corver (2010) has undertaken for HEFCE on the trends in young participation in higher education in England. He found that if you were a young person from a disadvantaged area you would have a one in five chance of progressing to higher education compared to one in two for those from the most advantaged neighbourhoods. The research also demonstrated that a key barrier to access is prior attainment. For a given A-level performance, the chances of going to university do not differ between social classes. Indeed, the evidence from the 2006 rise in fees is instructive here. Despite the predictions that participation by students from lower socioeconomic classes would fall, in fact the data show that not only did participation from the lowest socioeconomic classes increase more in relative terms from 2003–9 (by 26 per cent compared to 4 per cent) than did participation from the highest socioeconomic classes, but it also increased more in absolute terms (by 4 per cent compared to 2 per cent).

However, one worrying trend concerns the institutions that students from lower socioeconomic backgrounds go to. Despite the significant increase in their participation noted above, it has been focused in the less selective institutions. In this light, Fair Access (who goes to which university) remains a potent political issue every bit as much as does Widening Participation (increasing the overall level of participation in universities). The results of OFFA's negotiations with institutions published in July 2011 shows that the more selective institutions will be paying a lot more of the increased 'fee' income in bursaries and fee waivers than will the less selective institutions, an outcome intended to rectify the existing pattern of student recruitment.

Research by the Sutton Trust (2004; 2008) also demonstrates the problem starkly. It has estimated that Fair Access affects roughly 3,000 state school pupils each year, whereas widening participation refers to about 360,000 sixteen-year-olds each year who do not obtain five good GCSEs between A* and C including English and Maths (only 53 per cent of sixteen-year-olds currently attain that level) and are therefore unable to progress to A level. Around 60,000 of those were in the top 20 per cent at some time in their school education but do not go on to higher education by the age of nineteen. Furthermore, nearly 60 per cent of children from higher socioeconomic groups achieve five good GCSEs compared to only 31 per cent from lower socioeconomic groups and just 16 per cent of those eligible for free school meals.

I believe that all students deserve a level playing field in terms of opportunities to enter higher education and benefit from it. Participation in HE must be about the ability of a student to fulfil their potential and not just a reward based on past achievement. To do this means moving beyond just looking at academic achievement. Should other additional factors be considered when selecting students, if so how, when and to what extent? And should this include making an offer that can differ in some way from the 'standard' offer for a course?

I am clear where I stand on this. I believe that we should use such contextual data. I think that this will be increasingly important in the new world. But it is a fiercely contentious issue and we need more evidence that supports using it. It is important that contextual information is only used as part of a holistic form of assessment. I would not propose using school performance data in isolation in the offer-making process, but to take account of it in deciding the appropriate level of offer within the published offer range. This means that we primarily support excellence. In the future, if universities are to become more sophisticated in the use of contextual admissions, we will need access to more robust information that is consistent, reliable and accessible. And it is encouraging that this evidence base is now expanding.

Like many, I was the first in my family to go to university. I have never forgotten that, and I never will. Neither have I forgotten my German teacher at grammar school, who told my parents that the best job I could ever expect to get would be to sweep the floors in Norvic shoe factory in Norwich. Thanks to my parents, and to one inspirational teacher in particular (Mr Shearing), I did get the encouragement needed to raise my aspirations. And education has played a major role in making me the person I am today. If it had not been for my education, I would not have had the life opportunities I have had. Not many of my peers went to university, and not a day goes by without me reminding myself of how lucky I was to have had that encouragement. Part of the reason why I do what I do is because I am committed, like so many teachers, lecturers and professors, to helping create the same possibilities for others.

Through the seismic changes we are currently witnessing, all of us must work tirelessly to ensure that this remains the case. I fervently hope that universities can continue to be – and indeed can increase their role as – critical agents of social mobility in the future. I see no reason why this cannot be the case, especially if all concerned work together to inform prospective students about the realities of the new funding regime. In this light the work of Martin Lewis in publicizing the 'facts' of the new student funding package has been particularly interesting. Of course, we need to wait to see the outcomes of the new student funding package on participation, but I remain strongly of the view that if the actual proposals are communicated, rather than the myths, typified by a focus on 'fees' as distinct from 'graduate repayments', the applicants should not be put off going to university. Having said all of which, I expect applications to dip in 2012 before picking up again thereafter. And, do remember that over 200,000 applicants through UCAS did not end up going to university in 2010 (the evidence suggests that upwards of 97,000 did not succeed in getting a place).

Conclusion

I write this piece just a few days before I step down as President of Universities UK. It would be a massive understatement to say that it has been an eventful, stressful and challenging time at which to serve in that position. It has also been unavoidably controversial. Yet I truly believe that the future is bright for our universities. I have confidence that students will continue to see the value of that offer once the new funding regime is in place. I am sure, too, that it will drive major changes to the way the sector operates but that is something we should embrace and welcome. We need government to make the right choices to support participation, support research and develop skills. And we should aim to create a university system that is even more relevant and even better equipped to deliver the best possible higher education to the students of tomorrow. Working towards these goals has meant that UUK as an organization, through its Board, and myself as its President has had to take some very difficult decisions. It has not been possible to satisfy all our members, nor to come up with an outcome that suited all interested parties in the debates over the future of HE in this county. I only hope that in this brief afterword I have explained the rationale behind the choices I have made in terms of which policies to support. The most complicated, and fraught, choice was whether to believe that the new government meant what it said over the level of cuts to teaching funding. I was absolutely convinced that they did mean it, and from that conviction my policy positions followed.

I do not expect my arguments to convince those who disagree with the positions I've taken, but please do believe one statement: whatever I have done as President of UUK it was intended to strengthen, not weaken, the UK's universities; to make them more internationally competitive; to make them stronger financially; and, above all, to promote greater social inclusion. If I was right in believing the government's position on the reductions in funding of universities, then the crucial question becomes how would those who disagree with the policies adopted by UUK have achieved these objectives?

Notes

Introduction

1   Following the devolution of powers to national assemblies in Scotland, Wales and Northern Ireland in 2000, the UK national Parliament has jurisdiction only over education policies in England (there being no separate assembly for England independent of the UK parliament, as is the case for the other constituent countries in the UK). The assemblies in Wales and Scotland have declared that they will not enact the policies being described here, although they will have consequences for higher education in these jurisdictions.

2   At the time of writing the success of such measures is unclear, although it seems that many universities will pull back from their earlier intention to charge the higher fee, in which case the extent of cuts to the sector will be correspondingly more severe. A White Paper on higher education was issued in June 2011 with proposals for a 'core and margin' system of student quotas designed to bring fees down to around £7,500 for most institutions.

3   This is also reinforced by the White Paper, *Putting Students at the Heart of Higher Education* (White Paper 2011). For a detailed response to the White Paper, see Campaign for the Public University (Campaign for the Public University and Other Groups 2011).

4   In fact, the numbers pursuing degree courses in 1962 was small if only universities and full-time education are counted – approx 4 per cent of the age cohort – but rises to 15 per cent if all institutions and routes are counted (Robbins Report 1963: para 49). For the Robbins Committee, this was indicative both of the depth of the demand for higher education and of status differences associated with the different routes.

5   It is significant that the government also drastically curtailed the 'Educational Maintenance Allowance' designed to support young people to stay on in secondary education after the age of sixteen (when compulsory secondary education ceases).

6   This is the case with US private universities, where fees are significantly
       higher than is currently proposed in England, but where a significant
       proportion of the fee is used to enhance the 'status claims' of the
       institution and for research, each of which is necessary to establish the
       value of the education received as a 'positional good' (see Hotson 2011).

7   Lord Robbins himself came to advocate student loans, but he did not do
       so in the context of recommending the marketization of higher education
       (see Robbins 1980).

8   Reference to cynicism is apt in that the only research commissioned as
       part of the Browne Report was an attitude survey that showed wide
       public support for publicly funded higher education and that student
       fees should meet only a proportion of the cost. This research was not
       reported by the Browne Report.

9   98 per cent of mothers of children born in 2000 want their child to go to
       university (Wolf 2011).

Chapter 1 The Idea of a Public University

1   Indeed, neither Kerr's commentaries on higher education nor those of the
       Robbins Report (Robbins Report 1963) at more or less the same time
       can be understood outside those assumptions. See, for example, Kerr
       (1969) in which a 'multi-dimensional' society (with clear parallels to the
       'multiversity') is set out.

2   Of course, the decline of academic life as a 'vocation' is associated with
       the rise of 'vocational' higher education.

3   For example, the University of Birmingham was founded in 1901 around
       a Faculty of Commerce and a Faculty of Engineering (together with
       provision in modern languages for commercial purposes), in much the
       same way as the University of Nottingham's satellite campuses at Ningbo
       in China and in Malaysia are today, with little concern for the university
       as an instrument of culture, democracy and public debate.

4   The affordability of higher education is partly fees and partly living
       costs. Where the risk of indebtedness during study is high, part-time
       working becomes necessary, and students seek to reduce their costs by
       attending their 'local' university. 'Selective' universities tend to draw their
       students from further afield and, thus, applications are more likely to be

determined by the ability to pay.

5   It should be evident that the latter problem is not resolved by the principle of 'student choice' guided by employment aspirations. The latter would encourage problematic specialization just as much as the academic concern with disciplinary reproduction. As Robbins (1980) observed, the expansion of higher education brought about a requirement for a greater breadth in education and less specialization.

6   See Boltanski and Chiapello (2005) for a discussion of how counter-cultural values of the 1960s have been incorporated into the legitimation and justification of contemporary capitalism more generally.

7   This is a situation that will be reproduced in the British context, where a small elite group of universities are able to charge premium fees and have their eye on the lifting of the fee cap in order to charge fees equivalent to those of the US 'ivy league' colleges. See Hotson 2011.

8   Indeed, the proposed reforms align universities with a 'divided' secondary school system made up of 'selective' and 'independent' (or private) schools and non-selective state schools. Ironically, if there is a 'vision' behind the current reforms, it would seem to use 'market shock' to bring into being the 'three tier' California public university system initiated by Kerr – community college or further education college, state university and research university – whereas it is precisely the market that has undermined that system in California.

9   Robert Nelson (2001) has recently argued that economics should be thought of as a form of theological argument. He does not mean this unsympathetically, arguing that economics articulates the 'public interest' against the 'sectional interests' that otherwise beset government policy-making. The key article of faith is the competitive market as a mechanism that serves the public interest and allows outcomes determined by the subjective preferences of individuals.

10   See http://www.cabinetoffice.gov.uk/big-society [accessed 27 July 2011].

11   It has to be assumed that there is a market failure or, from the logic of the position, there is nothing for the 'Big Society' to do.

12   It is precisely this that Dewey suggests allows the understanding of the changing definition of the boundaries of what is conventionally regarded as private and public. The conventional definition of the 'private' is that of associated life that does not impinge with wider consequences upon others.

13   The transformation of university decision-making from collegial to
     hierarchical, managerial modes of organization is significant in the
     context of this quotation.

14   Thus, while the government claims that its recent budget is 'progressive'
     with regard to its social impact, the Institute of Fiscal Studies has shown
     that the burden falls mainly on the poor and that it is regressive (see
     Browne and Levell 2010).

Chapter 2 Redefining the Public University: Global and National Contexts

1   Data on the expansion of managerial ranks can be found at the
     homepage of Rona-Tas, http://weber.ucsd.edu/~aronatas/. On inequalities
     see, for example, Samuels 2010.

2   This is also one the implications of the proposed reforms of the French
     university system – autonomy handed to the university combined
     with funding cuts and, at the same time, intensified state regulation of
     centrally distributed research moneys.

3   This is a point made by Ron Amann who was the Chief Executive
     of the Social Science Research Council (1994–9) and before that he
     held a Chair at the University of Birmingham, specializing in Soviet
     science policy and the politics of economic reform in centrally planned
     economies (see Amann 2003).

4   This table is parallel to the one associated with Ernest Boyer (Boyer
     1997) which has four types of scholarship: discovery and application
     are extended to include teaching and integrative. Professional includes
     discovery but much more, application corresponds to policy, integrative
     corresponds to but is more limited than critical while teaching occurs
     in all four forms of knowledge. The big difference is the attempt to
     understand the relations of interdependence and antagonism in a field of
     domination that is the university system.

5   Thus, I am not defining the public university by open access for students,
     nor am I am even defining it by the source of its funds. A public
     university, as defined here, can be privately funded, usually, however, as
     a 'not-for-profit' organization. By itself, privatization need not imply the
     commodification of the production, dissemination and consumption of
     knowledge.

6   The four knowledges also correspond to Robert Merton's four dimensions of the ethos of science (Merton 1973): universalism that governs professional knowledge; disinterestedness that governs policy knowledge; organized scepticism that governs critical knowledge; and communism that governs public access. What Merton did not develop, however, are the contradictory and interdependent relations among these four moments.

7   Sari Hanafi (2011) has spoken evocatively of the dilemma as a choice between, on the one hand, publishing locally and perishing globally and, on the other hand, publishing globally and perishing locally.

8   This is knowledge increasingly advanced outside the university in such entities as 'think tanks' that are multidisciplinary and geared to policy questions.

Chapter 3 Open Unversities: A Vision for the Public University in the Twenty-first Century

1   The University Grants Committee, an arm's-length body to advise on the distribution of public funds to universities, started work in 1919. It was replaced in 1989 by the Universities Funding Council and in 1992 by Higher Education Funding Councils for England, Wales and Scotland.

2   It should be obvious that this is not to lose sight of mature students, but simply to recognize that at undergraduate level school-leavers make up the vast majority of students.

3   The February 2011 Universities UK report is a recent reminder of the importance of these identities and problems. See Universities UK, 'Freedom of Speech on Campus: Rights and Responsibilities in UK Universities', *Universities UK*, http://www.universitiesuk.ac.uk [accessed 21 August 2011].

4   See David Cameron's 'Big Society' speech on 19 July 2010 and his interview in the *Telegraph*, 21 February 2011. For the emphasis on responsibility as the basis of the big society see his 'Big Society' speech of 14 February 2011. Both speeches are available at http://www.number10. gov.uk.

5   Many people, from a variety of perspectives, have denounced the RAE for encouraging short-termism, narrow focus and an emphasis on quantitative indicators (prestige of the journal, number of pages, number

of citations) over the intellectual and scholarly qualities of the work. See, for example, Richard Baggaley of Princeton University Press (Baggaley 2007) and John Davis, former Warden of All Souls (Davis 1999). For a good summary of these arguments, see Head 2011.

Chapter 4 Science as a Public Good

1   In their book, *The Republic of Engagement*, Salter and his co-authors (Salter, Tartari, D'Este and Neely 2010) note that only 21 per cent of the physicists they surveyed had been involved in the creation of a commercial venture based on their research. This figure fell to 9 per cent for mathematicians. Moreover, only 16 per cent of physicists and 6 per cent of mathematicians expressed an interest in starting a new business 'within the next three years'. The highest percentage (30 per cent) of academics who responded positively was found amongst chemical engineers. There are strong disciplinary differences with regard to entrepreneurial activity but it is clear that the majority of academic scientists do not see entrepreneurship as an important attribute to develop in their career.

2   I avoid the use of the terms 'excellent' and 'excellence' throughout this chapter. Both are now unfortunately part of the lexicon of vacuous jargon that pervades university management. See Readings 1996 on the status of 'excellence' as an 'empty signifier'.

3   Merton later added one other norm, originality, to generate the 'CUDOS' acronym.

4   PPARC was merged with the Council for the Central Laboratory of the Research Councils (CCLRC) to form the Science and Technology Facilities Council (STFC) in 2007. STFC has had what might best be called a turbulent history since its inception.

5   Callon makes a fascinating argument regarding technological stagnation in a 'perfectly privatizable' funding regime (which he describes as 'the market smothers the market') (Callon 2003).

6   It is perhaps worth noting at this point that the distinction I draw between 'Mertonian' and 'utilitarian' science is distinct from the so-called Mode 1/Mode 2 division put forward by Gibbons *et al.* (1994), although sharing some features in common. In particular, there is no reason why science conforming to the Mertonian norms need not be interdisciplinary

(a feature usually ascribed only to Mode 2 research). Nanoscience – the intensely interdisciplinary field of research field in which I work – was described by Vogt *et al.* (2007) as an exemplar of Mode 2 research in that it ostensibly has a strong emphasis on 'how', i.e. application-driven, rather than 'why' questions. For the reasons outlined in Moriarty (2008) and Mowery (2011), however, casting the entire nanotechnology/nanoscience field as Mode 2 research is a bold and unjustified assertion.

7   Particularly if those funding bodies claim to be bound by the Haldane principle of distancing decisions related to science funding from direct government control. Edgerton's excellent account of the development of the Haldane principle (Edgerton 2009) shows that the history of what many see as a fundamental tenet of UK funding policy is remarkably different from that assumed by the vast majority of academics, politicians and policy-makers. Notwithstanding Edgerton's important analysis, the Haldane principle is widely understood to represent the protection of publicly funded academic science from government pressure driven by political expediency.

8   On the 'expert' vs 'sceptical' norms, one is put in mind of Richard Feynman's one sentence definition of science: 'Science is the belief in the ignorance of experts.'

9   As I was completing this chapter, news broke that the Arts and Humanities Research Council (AHRC) had allegedly allocated a significant amount of its budget for research into the 'Big Society' (the rather nebulous ideology *du jour* of the Conservative-Liberal Democrat coalition). This development mirrors EPSRC's transition to a 'sponsor' of research but is arguably even more disturbing in that it apparently represents an unprecedented perversion of the ethos of academic research so as to align the policies of a research council with political objectives. Note that direct government interference is not required for this to happen. The research councils, in their (otherwise laudable) aim to secure as much funding as possible from the Treasury in each round of the Comprehensive Spending Review, are always keen to show alignment of their funding strategies with government policy.

10   The comments that follow were all posted as part of the RCUK consultation exercise, but are no longer maintained on its website. They are now part of the author's personal archive and are available on request.

11   RCUK argues that applicants are asked to describe the broad
      socioeconomic impact, rather than just the economic impact, of
      their research. This is indeed the case but RCUK did not introduce
      the requirement for an impact statement because they suddenly
      became concerned that there were not enough academics involved in
      public engagement/outreach activities or the broader societal impact
      of university research. The impact statement was introduced as a
      direct response to the Warry Report and serves as an impetus for the
      development of a much stronger entrepreneurial culture in academia. To
      suggest otherwise is naive in the extreme.

Chapter 5 The Politics of Publicly-funded Social Research

1   This chapter draws on material in King (1997); King (1998).

2   http://www.esrc.ac.uk/news-and-events/15733/refiningstrategicpriorities
      [accessed 27 July 2011]. By this it seems to mean that decisions will
      continue to be made on the basis of peer review, but that review will
      consider the degree of fit with the priorities and their potential impact.

3   For example, Andrew Shonfield's influential book, *Modern Capitalism*
      (Shonfield 1965) and the Labour Party statement, *Labour and the
      Scientific Revolution* (Labour Party 1963).

4   The committee convened a key seminar with leading academics in social
      science in January 1964 to discuss its proposed recommendations.

5   Joseph's leadership chances vanished after he delivered a speech on 19
      October 1974 in Edgbaston, taken by many critics to be sympathetic to
      outdated eugenicist arguments, with such turns of phrase as 'our human
      stock is threatened'. In a wide-ranging speech this latter phrase alluded
      to the issue of adolescent birth rates, and he also voiced concern about
      the intellectualism of universities.

6   An important guide is Posner (Posner 2006). He was Chairman (1979–
      83) of the SSRC during the period of review in the early 1980s.

7   The terms of reference were threefold: '(i) Which areas, if any, of the
      SSRC's work should be done at the expense of the ultimate consumer
      rather than the Exchequer; (ii) Which areas, rightly supported by the
      Exchequer, could be done at least as well and as economically by other
      bodies, who would receive payment from the public purse either on
      a once-and-for-all or recurrent basis. The bodies concerned should be

identified; and (iii) Which areas, if any, at present supported by the Exchequer through other bodies could be better covered by the SSRC' (Rothschild Report 1982: 9).

8   This request for no reduction in real terms of the SSRC budget for three years was rejected by the Secretary of State on the grounds that, 'the Government must maintain its right to review public expenditure from year to year. But there is a second reason. The Government believes that within the Science Vote relatively higher priority should be given to work in the natural sciences – particularly to sustain a flow of the best young research talent – and relatively lower priority to work in social studies. I therefore wish to see over the next three years a corresponding and steadily rising redeployment within the Science Budget of some of your Council's resources, this money to be applied – as the Advisory Board for the Research Councils may advise – towards the Government's aim of providing money for new blood for research in the natural sciences particularly in universities.' Statement in the House of Commons, 18 October 1982, reading from his letter to the Chairman of the SSRC, 14 October 1982.

9   This Unit had been the subject of particularly negative criticism for its research as left wing, a characterization wholly rejected.

10   Hansard (1982), 'House of Lords Debate, 30 June 1982', *Hansard*, London: Hansard, 432: 288.

11   Hansard (1982), 'House of Lords Debate, 30 June 1982', *Hansard*, London: Hansard, 432: 292.

12   Hansard (1982), 'House of Lords Debate, 30 June 1982', *Hansard*, London: Hansard, 432: 295.

13   As guides to understanding the sources and shape of the current crisis compare for example the approach in MacKenzie 2009 with Koo 2008 and Krippner 2011.

14   April 2010 with an outstanding group of economists presenting papers. The papers do an excellent job of analysing the crisis and, given the calibre of scholars associated with the Institute, the road map for future research is likely to exciting and original, although this was not yet set out. The website (http://ineteconomics.org) states: 'The havoc wrought by our recent global financial crisis has vividly demonstrated the deficiencies in our outdated current economic theories, and shown the need for new economic thinking – right now. INET is supporting this fundamental

shift in economic thinking through research funding, community
building, and spreading the word about the need for change.'

Chapter 6 The Religion of Inequality

1   The Labour Force Survey is a continuous sample survey of the UK
population, interviewing around 120,000 per calendar quarter (Office
for National Statistics. Social and Vital Statistics Division and Northern
Ireland Statistics and Research Agency, Central Survey Unit 2010). It is
used to provide regular statistics on unemployment and worklessness, as
well as more general statistics on the labour force.

2   The median represents the pay of the person who is halfway in the
distribution of earners – half earn more, and half earn less. It is less
subject than the arithmetic mean (the 'average') to being affected by a
few very high figures.

3   A further 2 per cent were unsure how to respond.

4   The full quotation being, 'Want is one only of five giants on the road of
reconstruction and in some ways the easiest to attack. The others are
Disease, Ignorance, Squalor and Idleness' (Beveridge Report 1942: Part 1,
para. 8). Want, to be tackled through social insurance, was of course the
main theme of the Beveridge Report.

Afterword: A Positive Future for Higher Education in England

1   See the announcements of intended widening participation
arrangements, published by OFFA on 11 July 2011.

Bibliography

Amman, R. (2003), 'A Sovietological view of modern Britain', *Political Quarterly*, 74 (4): 468–80.

Anderson, M.S., Ronning, E.A., DeVries, R. and Martinson, B.C. (2010), 'Extending the Mertonian norms: scientists' subscription to norms of research', *Journal of Higher Education*, 81: 366–93.

Archer, L. and Leathwood, C. (2003), 'Identities, inequalities and higher education', in Louise Archer, Merryn Hutchings and Alistair Ross (eds), *Higher Education and Social Class: Issues of Inclusion and Exclusion*, London: RoutledgeFalmer.

Atherton, G., McNeill, J. and Okonkwo, J. (2010), *What Price Fairness? The Impact of Finance and Cost on Young People's Views on Higher Education Participation*, London: Aimhigher.

Atkinson, A. and Harrison, G. (1978), *The Distribution of Personal Wealth in Britain*, Cambridge: Cambridge University Press.

Atkinson, A. and Salverda, W. (2003), *Top Incomes in the Netherlands and the United Kingdom over the Twentieth Century*, Amsterdam: Amsterdam Institute for Advanced Labour Studies, http://www.uva-aias.net/uploaded_files/publications/WP14.pdf [accessed 23 August 2011].

Atkinson, A. B. (2007), 'Top incomes in the United Kingdom over the twentieth century', in A. Atkinson and T. Piketty (eds), *Top Incomes over the Twentieth Century: A Contrast Between Continental European and English Speaking Countries*, Oxford: Oxford University Press, 82–140.

Baggaley, R. (2007), 'How the RAE is smothering "Big Idea" books', *Times Higher Education*, 25 May.

Baimbridge, M. and Simpson, C. (1996), 'Rewards to academia: the remuneration of vice chancellors and principals', *Applied Economics*, 28 (6): 631–9.

Balconi, M., Brusoni, S. and Orsenigo, L. (2010), 'In defence of the linear model: an essay', *Research Policy*, 39: 1–13.

Battelle (2009), 'Global R&D Funding Forecast', *Battelle*, http://www.battelle.org/news/pdfs/2009RDFundingfinalreport.pdf [accessed 21 August 2011].

Beveridge Report (1942), *Social Insurance and Allied Services,* Report by Sir William Beveridge. London: HMSO.

Bikbov, A. (n.d.), 'How Russian universities became the future of world education', *Universities in Crisis Blog*, http://www.isa-sociology.org/universities-in-crisis/?p=441 [accessed 3 July 2011].

Blackstone, Baroness (2010), 'House of Lords Debate, 27 October 2010', *Hansard*, London: Hansard, col. 1238. Available at: http://www.publications.parliament.uk/pa/ld201011/ldhansrd/text/101027-0001.htm#10102762000053 [accessed 27 July 2011].

Blanden, J., Gregg, P. and Machin, S. (2005), *Intergenerational Mobility in Europe and North America*, London: Sutton Trust.

Blanden, J. and Machin, S. (2007), *Recent Changes in Intergenerational Mobility. Report for the Sutton Trust*, London: Sutton Trust.

Blanden, J. (2009), 'How much can we learn from international comparisons of intergenerational mobility?', London: Centre for the Economics of Education Discussion Paper 111. Available at: http://cee.lse.ac.uk/ceedps/ceedp111.pdf [accessed 30 August 2011].

Bok, D. (2003), *Universities in the Marketplace*, Princeton, NJ: Princeton University Press.

Boltanski, L. and Chiapello, E. (2005), *The New Spirit of Capitalism*, trans. Gregory Elliott, London: Verso.

Boulton, G. and Lucas, C. (2008), *What Are Universities For?*, Edinburgh/ Oxford: League of European Research Universities, http://www.leru.org/ files/general/What are universities for 28September 2008.pdf [accessed 21 August 2011].

Boyer, E. (1997), *Scholarship Reconsidered: Priorities of the Professoriate*, New York, NY: Jossey-Bass.

Breen, R. and Goldthorpe, J.H. (1999), 'Class inequality and meritocracy: a critique of Saunders and an alternative analysis', *British Journal of Sociology*, 50: 1–27.

Browne, J. and Levell, P. (2010), 'The distributional effect of tax and benefit reforms to be introduced between June 2010 and April 2014: a revised assessment', IFS Briefing Note 108, http://www.ifs.org.uk/bns/bn108.pdf [accessed 27 May 2011].

Browne, J. (2011) *The Impact of Tax and Benefit Changes to be Implemented in April 2011*, London: Institute for Fiscal Studies.

Browne Report (2010), *Securing a Sustainable Future for Higher Education: An Independent Review of Higher Education Funding and Student Finance*, London: Independent Review of Higher Education Funding and Student Finance. Available at: http://www.independent.gov.uk/browne-report [accessed 21 August 2011].

Bufton, S. (2003), 'The "Lifeworld" of the university student: habitus and social class', *Journal of Phenomenological Psychology*, 34 (2): 207–34.

Bush, V. (1945), *Science, The Endless Frontier. A Report to the President by Vannevar Bush, Director of the Office of Scientific Research and Development*, Washington, DC: United States Government Printing Office.

Cadwalladr, C. (2008), 'It's the clever way to power', *Guardian*, 16 March. Available at: http://www.guardian.co.uk/education/2008/mar/16/ highereducation.news [accessed 30 August 2011].

Callender, C. and Jackson, J. (2008), 'Does the fear of debt constrain choice of university and subject of study?', *Studies in Higher Education*, 33 (4).

Callon, M. (1994), 'Is science a public good? (Fifth Mullins Lecture, Virginia Polytechnic Institute, 23 March 1993)', *Science, Technology, and Human Values*, 19: 395–424.

Calvert, J. (2006), 'What's special about basic research?', *Science, Technology and Human Values*, 31: 199–220.

Campaign for the Public University and Other Groups (2011), *Putting Vision Back into Higher Education: A Response to the White Paper*. Available at: http://publicuniversity.org.uk/wp-content/uploads/2011/07/Response_to_White_Paper_Final.pdf [accessed 27 July 2011].

Clapham Report (1946), *Report of the Committee on the Provision for Social and Economic Research*, London: HMSO, Cmd 6808.

Clegg, N. (2010), 'Inequality becomes injustice when it is passed on, generation to generation', *Guardian*, 22 November.

Collini, S. (2010), 'Browne's gamble', *London Review of Books*, 32 (21) (4 November). Available at: http://www.lrb.co.uk/v32/n21/stefan-collini/brownes-gamble (accessed 25 July 2011).

Committee on Social Studies (1964), 'Report on Seminar held on 13–14 January 1964, Part VI "On the Present State of Knowledge in the Social Sciences"', London: Committee on Social Studies.

Committee on Social Studies Minutes (1964), 'Minutes of Proceedings at a Seminar of Users, 9 November 1964', London: Committee on Social Studies, PRO Folder ED 144–5, 23590.

Confederation of British Industry (2011), *Building for Growth: Business Priorities for Education and Skills – Education and Skills Survey 2011*, London: Confederation of British Industry, May.

Corbyn, Z. (2009), 'Research councils unveil future vision', *Times Higher Education*, 9 April.

Corver, M. (2010), *Trends in Young Participation in Higher Education: Core Results for England*, London: Higher Education Funding Council for England, January.

Crockett, R. (1994), *Thinking the Unthinkable: Think Tanks and the Economic Counter Revolution*, London: Harper Collins.

Dahl, R. (2001), *Boy: Tales of Childhood*, London: Puffin.

Davis, J. (1999), 'Administering creativity', *Anthropology Today*, 15 (2).

Dearing Report (1997), *Report of the National Committee of Inquiry into Higher Education*, London: DFEE. Available at: http://www.leeds.ac.uk/educol/ncihe/sumrep.htm [accessed 25 July 2011].

Dewey, J. (1927), *The Public and its Problems*, Athens, OH: Ohio University Press.

Dorling, D. (2010), *Injustice: Why Social Inequality Persists*, Bristol: PolicyPress.

Eagleton, T. (2010), 'The death of universities', *Guardian*, 18 December.

Edgerton, D. (2009), 'The "Haldane principle" and other invented traditions in science policy', *History and Policy*, http://www.historyandpolicy.org/papers/policy-paper-88.html [accessed 31 March 2011].

EPSRC (2011), *EPSRC Delivery Plan 2011-2015*, Swindon: Engineering and Physical Sciences Research Council. Available at: http://www.epsrc.ac.uk/SiteCollectionDocuments/Publications/corporate/

EPSRCDeliveryPlan2011-15.pdf [accessed 30 August 2011].

Esping-Andersen, G. (1990), *The Three Worlds of Welfare Capitalism*, Cambridge: Polity Press.

ESRC (2005), *SSRC/ESRC: The First Forty Years*, London: Economic and Social Research Council, http://www.esrc.ac.uk/_images/ESRC-40-years_tcm8-6369.pdf [accessed 22 August 2011].

ESRC (2010), *ESRC Delivery Plan 2011–2015*, Swindon: Economic and Social Research Council. Available at: http://www.esrc.ac.uk/publications/deliveryplan/ [accessed 30 August 2011].

Fabrizio, K.R. (2007), 'University patenting and the pace of industrial innovation', *Industrial and Corporate Change*, 16: 505–34.

Finlayson, G. and Hayward, D. (2010) *Education towards Heteronomy: UK University Reform since 1978*, http://www.sussex.ac.uk/Users/jgf21/eth finalversion.pdf [accessed 30 March 2011].

Fish, S. (2010), 'The value of higher education made literal', *New York Times*, 13 December.

Gibbons, M., Limoges, C., Nowotny, H., Schwarztman, S., Scott, P. and Trow, M. (1994), *The New Production of Knowledge: The Dynamics of Science and Research in Contemporary Societies*, London: Sage.

Giddens, A. (1991), *Modernity and Self-Identity*, Stanford, CA: Stanford University Press.

Glass, D.V. (1950), 'The application of social research', *British Journal of Sociology*, 1 (1).

Goldthorpe, J. and Mills, C. (2008), 'Trends in intergenerational class mobility in modern Britain: evidence from national surveys, 1972–2005', *National Institute Economic Review*, 205 (1): 83–100.

Gove, M. (2010), 'Address to the Conservative Party conference', *DeHavilland*, http://www.dehavilland.co.uk [accessed 22 August 2011].

Green, A., Janmaat, G. and Cheng, H. (2011), 'Social cohesion: converging and diverging trends', *National Institute Economic Review*, 215 (January), London: NIESR.

Green, F., Machin, S., Murphy, R. and Zhu, Y. (2010), *The Changing Economic Advantage from Private School*, CEE discussion papers, CEEDP0115, London: Centre for the Economics of Education, London School of Economics and Political Science, http://eprints.lse.ac.uk/28288/ [accessed 23 August 2011].

Greenberg, D.S. (2007), *Science for Sale*, Chicago, IL: University of Chicago Press.

Guardian (2010a) 'Oxbridge's class divide raises food for thought', *Guardian*, 18 September, http://www.guardian.co.uk/theguardian/2010/sep/18/oxfordcambridge-university-free-meals [accessed 23 August 2011].

Guardian (2010b), 'Working-class revolution not reaching "posh" universities', *Guardian*, 28 September, http://www.guardian.co.uk/education/2010/sep/28/working-class-students-posh-universities [accessed 23 August 2011].

Guri-Rosenblit, S., Sebkova, H. and Teichler, U. (2007), *Massification and Diversity of Higher Education Systems: Interplay of Complex Dimensions*, Paris: UNESCO.

Halsey, A.H. (1994), 'Sociology as political arithmetic', *British Journal of Sociology*, 45: 427–44.

Hanafi, S. (2011), 'University systems in the Arab East: Publish globally and perish locally vs. publish locally and perish globally', *Current Sociology*, 59 (3).

Haux, R. Jawad and M. Kilkey, M (eds), *In Defence of Welfare: The Impacts of the Spending Review*, London: Social Policy Association.

Head, S. (2011), 'The grim threat to British universities', *The New York Review of Books*, 13 January.

HEFCE (2010), 'Research Excellence Framework: Impact pilot exercise – example case studies from Physics', London: Higher Education Funding Council for England, November. Available at: http://www.hefce.ac.uk/research/ref/impact/ [accessed 30 August 2011].

Hess, D.J. (1997), *Science Studies: An Advanced Introduction*, New York, NY: New York University Press.

Heyworth Report (1965), *Report of the Committee on Social Studies*, London: HMSO, Cmnd 2660.

Hills, J. (2004), *Inequality and the State*, Oxford: Oxford University Press.

HM Revenue and Customs (2011), *Distribution of Personal Wealth*. Available at: http://www.hmrc.gov.uk/stats/personal_wealth/menu.htm [accessed 30 August 2011].

HM Treasury (2010a), *2010 Budget*, HC 61, London: The Stationery Office.

HM Treasury (2010b), *Spending Review*, Cmd 7942, London: The Stationery Office.

Hotson, H. (2011), 'Don't look to the Ivy League', *London Review of Books*, 33 (10) (19 May). Available at: http://www.lrb.co.uk/v33/n10/howard-hotson/dont-look-to-the-ivy-league [accessed 27 July 2011].

Hutton, W. (2007), 'Class still rules our college life', *Observer*, 23 September.

Iannelli, C. and Paterson, L. (2006) 'Social mobility in Scotland since the middle of the twentieth century', *Sociological Review*, 54 (3): 520–45.

IMF (2010), 'International Monetary Fund World Economic Outlook Database', October 2010. Available at: http://www.imf.org/external/ns/cs.aspx?id=28 [accessed 30 August 2011].

James, A., Horton, R., Collingridge, D., McConnell, J. and Butcher, J. (2004), 'The Lancet's policy on conflicts of interest', *Lancet*, 363: 2–3.

Jasanoff, S. (2004), 'Ordering knowledge, ordering society', in Sheila Jasanoff (ed.), *States of Knowledge: The Co-Production of Science and Social Order*, London: Routledge.

Jump, P., (2010), 'Impact scepticism', *Times Higher Education*, 18 May.

Kellog, D. (2006), 'Toward a post-academic science policy: scientific communication and the collapse of the Mertonian norms', *International Journal of Communications, Law and Policy* (Online), 11, http://www.ijclp.net/files/ijclp_web-doc_1-11-2006.pdf [accessed 30 August 2011].

Kenney, M. and Patton, D. (2009), 'Reconsidering the Bayh-Dole Act and the current university invention ownership model', *Research Policy*, 38 (9): 1407–22.

Kerr, C. (1969), *Marshall, Marx and Modern Times: The Multi-Dimensional Society*, Cambridge: Cambridge University Press.

Kerr, C. (2001 [1963]), *The Uses of the University*, 5th edition, Cambridge, MA: Harvard University Press.

King, D. (1997), 'Creating a funding regime for social research: the Heyworth Committee on Social Studies and the founding of the British SSRC', *Minerva*, 35.

King, D. (1998), 'The politics of social research: institutionalizing public funding regimes in the United States and Britain', *British Journal of Political Science*, 28.

Kirp, D. (2003), *Shakespeare, Einstein, and the Bottom Line*, Cambridge, MA: Harvard University Press.

Kleinman, D.L. (1995), *Politics on the Endless Frontier*, Durham, NC: Duke University Press.

Kline, S.J. and Rosenberg, N. (1986), 'An overview of innovation', in R. Landau and N. Rosenberg (eds), *The Positive Sum Strategy: Harnessing Technology for Economic Growth*, Washington, DC: National Academy Press.

Koo, R. C., *The Holy Grail of Macroeconomics: Lessons from Japan's Great Recession*, Hoboken, NJ: Wiley.

Krippner, G. R. (2011), *Capitalizing on Crisis: The Political Origins of the Rise of Finance*, Cambridge, MA: Harvard University Press.

Labour Party (1963), *Labour and the Scientific Revolution*, London: Labour Party.

Lambert, R. and Smith, S. (2009), 'Higher education's importance goes well beyond teaching', *Guardian*, 3 November.

Lammy, D. (2010), 'The Oxbridge whitewash', *Guardian*, 7 December: 28.

Langlands, A. (2005), *The Gateways to the Professions Report*, Nottingham: Department for Education and Skills Publications, http://www.bis.gov.uk/assets/biscore/corporate/migratedd/publications/g/gateways_to_the_professions_report.pdf [accessed 23 August 2011].

Langley, C. and Parkinson, S. (2009), *Science and the Corporate Agenda*, Folkestone: Scientists for Global Responsibility.

Larsen, O. (1992), *Milestones and Millstones: Social Science at the National Science Foundation*, New Brunswick, NJ: Transaction.

Leigh, A. (2007), 'How closely do top income shares track other measures of inequality?', *Economic Journal*, 117 (524): F619–F633.

Leitch, S. (2006), *Prosperity for All in the Global Economy – World Class Skills*, London: HMSO.

Lippmann, W. (1925), *The Phantom Public*, New York, NY: Macmillan.

Lynch, K. (2006), 'Neo-Liberalism and marketisation: the implications for higher education', *European Educational Research Journal*, 5 (1): 1–17.

MacInnes, J. (2009), 'Proposal to support and improve the teaching of quantitative research method at undergraduate level in the UK', Report to ESRC, London: Economic and Social Research Council, 29 December.

MacKenzie, D. (2009), *Material Markets: How Economic Agencies Are*

Constructed, Oxford: Oxford University Press.

Macmillan, L. (2009), *Social Mobility and the Professions – for Submission to the Panel for Fair Access to the Professions*, Bristol: CMPO.

Mamdani, M. (2007), *Scholars in the Marketplace*, Dakar, Senegal: Council for the Development of Social Science Research in Africa..

Mandler, P. (2011), 'While you were looking elsewhere … The Haldane principle and the government's research agenda for the arts and humanities', *Humanities Matter*, http://humanitiesmatter.wordpress.com/2011/01/30/while-you-were-looking-elsewhere...the-haldane-principle-and-thegovernment's-research-agenda-for-the-arts-and-humanities/ [accessed 21 August 2011].

Mangan, J., Hughes, A., Davies, P. and Slack, K. (2010), 'Fair access, achievement and geography: explaining the association between social class and students' choice of university', *Studies in Higher Education*, 35 (3): 335–50.

Marshall, T.H. (1992 [1950]), 'Citizenship and social class', in T.H. Marshall and T. Bottomore, (1992), *Citizenship and Social Class and Other Essays*, Cambridge: Cambridge University Press, 3–51.

Massey, D. (2006), 'Blackballed by Bush', *Contexts*, Winter.

McGettigan, A. (2010), 'New providers: The creation of a market in higher education', *Radical Philosophy*, 187 (May–June).

McKay, S. and Rowlingson, K. (2008), 'Social security and welfare reform', in M. Powell (ed.), *Modernising the Welfare State: The Blair Legacy*, Bristol: Policy Press, 53–72.

McKay, S. (2010), 'Where do we stand on inequality?', *Journal of Poverty and Social Justice*, 18 (1).

Merton, R. K. (1942), 'The normative structure of science', in Robert K. Merton, *The Sociology of Science: Theoretical and Empirical Investigations*, Chicago, IL: University of Chicago Press.

Milburn, A. (2009), *Unleashing Aspiration: The Final Report of the Panel on Fair Access to the Professions*, London: COI for the Panel on Fair to the Professions.

Mill, J.S. (1969) 'Bentham', in John Stuart Mill, *Essays on Ethics, Religion and Society*, ed. J.M. Robson, Toronto: University of Toronto Press.

Monbiot, G. (2010), 'Plan after plan fails to make Oxbridge access fair. There is another way', *Guardian*, 24 May.

Moriarty, P. (2008), 'Reclaiming academia from post-academia', *Nature Nanotechnology*, 3: 60–2.

Mowery, D.C. (2011), 'Nanotechnology and the US national innovation system: continuity and change', *Journal of Technology Transfer*, DOI 10.1007/s10961-011-9210-2.

Mulkay, M.J. (1976), 'Norms and ideology in science', *Social Science Information*, 15: 637–56.

National Centre for Social Research (various years), *British Social Attitudes Survey*, Colchester, Essex: UK Data Archive.

National Equality Panel (2010), *An Anatomy of Economic Inequality in the UK*, London: Government Equalities Office.

Nelson, R. H. (2001), *Economics as Religion: From Samuelson to Chicago and Beyond*, University Park, PA: Pennsylvania University Press.

Nelson, R.R. (2001), 'Observations on the post-Bayh–Dole rise of patenting at American universities', *Journal of Technology Transfer*, 26: 13–19.

Nelson, R.R. (2004), 'The market economy and the scientific commons', *Research Policy*, 33: 455–71.

Newfield, C. (2008), *The Unmaking of the Public University: The Forty Year Assault on the Middle Class*, Cambridge, MA: Harvard University Press.

Nicoletti, C. and Ermisch, J. (2007), 'Intergenerational earnings mobility: changes across cohorts in Britain', *B.E. Journal of Economic Analysis and Policy*, 7: 1–36.

Norwood, C. and Hope, A.H. (1909), *The Higher Education of Boys in England*, London: John Murray.

Nowotny, H., Scott, P. and Gibbons, M. (2001), *Re-Thinking Science*, Cambridge: Polity Press.

Nowotny, H. (2006), 'Real science is excellent science – how to interpret post-academic science, Mode 2 and the ERC', *Journal of Science Communication*, 5 (4).

OECD (2003), *Turning Science into Business. Patenting and Licensing at Public Research Organizations*, Paris: Organisation for Economic Co-operation and Development.

OECD (2007), *Education at a Glance – OECD Briefing Note for the UK*, Paris: OECD, http://www.oecd.org/dataoecd/22/36/39317646.pdf [accessed 23 August 2011].

OECD (2010), *Education at a Glance 2010*, Paris: OECD, September.

Office for National Statistics, Social and Vital Statistics Division and Northern Ireland Statistics and Research Agency, Central Survey Unit (2010), *Quarterly Labour Force Survey, July – September, 2010*, Colchester: UKData Archive.

O'Neill, O. (2002), *A Question of Trust*, Cambridge: Cambridge University Press.

O'Rourke, L., Caffrey, R. and Lester, A. (2010), *Bursting the Bubble: How the Browne Review Will Impact the Real World*, Merseyside: Aimhigher.

Paton, G. (2007), 'Education apartheid as private schools flood elite universities', *Daily Telegraph*, 27 November.

Pennell, H. and West, A. (2005), 'The impact of increased fees on participation in higher education in England', *Higher Education Quarterly*, 59: 127–37.

Polanyi, M. (1962), 'The republic of science', *Minerva*, 1: 54.

Posner, M. (2002), 'Social sciences under attack in the UK (1981–1983)', *La revue pour l'histoire du CNRS [En ligne]*, 7, http://histories-cnrs.revues.org/547 [accessed 22 August 2011].

Power, S. and Whitty, G. (2008), *Graduating and Gradations within the Middle Class: The Legacy of an Elite Higher Education*, Cardiff: Cardiff School of

Social Sciences Working Papers Series.

RCUK (2003), *Response to the Lambert Review of Business-University Collaboration*, London: Research Councils UK, http://www.hm-treasury.gov.uk/d/prcukdrdhleech150403.pdf [accessed 31 March 2011].

RCUK (2006), *Efficiency and Effectiveness of Peer Review: Consultation*, London: Research Councils UK, http://www.rcuk.ac.uk/documents/documents/prconsultation.pdf [accessed 31 March 2011].

RCUK (2007), *RCUK Efficiency and Value for Money of Peer Review Project*, London: Research Councils UK, http://www.rcuk.ac.uk/reviews/home/Pages/vfmpeerreview.aspx [accessed 31 March 2011].

RCUK (2009), *RCUK Knowledge Exchange and Impact*, London: Research Councils UK, http://www.rcuk.ac.uk/kei/Pages/home.aspx [accessed 31March 2011].

RCUK (2010), 'Top ten tips for completing the "pathways to impact" statement', *Research Councils UK* (Online), http://www.rcuk.ac.uk/kei/impacts/Pages/top10tips.aspx [accessed 31 March 2011].

RCUK (2011), 'Excellence with impact: intellectual property', *Research Councils UK* (Online), http://www.rcuk.ac.uk/kei/maximising/Pages/IntellectualProperty.aspx [accessed 1 August 2011].

Readings, B. (1996), *The University in Ruins*, Cambridge, MA: Harvard University Press.

Reay, D., Ball, S.J., David, M. and Davies, J. (2001), 'Choices of degree or degrees of choice? Social class, race and the higher education choice process', *Sociology*, 35 (4): 855–74.

Reay, D., David, M. and Ball, S. (2005), *Degrees of Choice: Social Class, Race and Gender in Higher Education*, Stoke-on-Trent: Trentham.

Reay, D., Crozier, G. and Clayton, J. (2009), 'Strangers in paradise: working class students in elite universities', *Sociology*, 43 (6): 1103–121.

Reay, D., Crozier, G. and James, D. (2011), *White Middle Class Identities and Urban Schooling*, London: Palgrave.

Reich, R. (1991), *The Work of Nations: Preparing Ourselves for 21st-Century Capitalism*, New York, NY: Vintage.

Research Councils UK (n.d.), 'Pathways to Impact', London: Research Councils UK, http://www.rcuk.ac.uk/kei/impacts/Pages/home.aspx [accessed 27 May 2011].

Robbins, Lord (1980), *Higher Education Revisited*, London: Macmillan.

Robbins Report (1963), *Higher Education: Report of the Committee appointed by the Prime Minister under the Chairmanship of Lord Robbins 1961–63*, London: HMSO, Cmnd 2154. Available at: http://www.educationengland.org.uk/documents/robbins/robbins00.html [accessed 25 July 2011].

Roberts, A. (2011), 'The end is not nigh', *Times Higher Education*, 3 March.

Roberts, K. (2010), 'Expansion of higher education and the implications for demographic class formation in Britain', *21st Century Society: Journal of the Academy of Social Sciences*, 5 (3): 215–28.

Rothschild Report (1982), *An Enquiry into the Social Science Research*

Council, London: HMSO, Cmnd 8554.

Rowlingson, K. and McKay, Stephen (2005), *Attitudes to Inheritance in Britain,* Bristol: Policy Press

Rowlingson, K. (2011), 'All in it together? Reflections on wealth, the wealthy and fairness', in N. Yeates, T. Haux, R. Jawad and M. Kilkey (eds), *In Defence of Welfare: The Impacts of the Spending Review*, London: Social Policy Association.

Sainsbury Report (2007), *The Race to the Top: A Review of Government's Science and Innovation Policies*, London: HMSO. Available at: http://www.rsc.org/images/sainsbury_review051007_tcm18-103116.pdf [accessed 27 July 2011].

Salter, A., Tartari, V., D'Este, P. and Neely A. (2010), *The Republic of Engagement: Exploring UK Academic Attitudes to Collaborating with Industry and Entrepreneurship*, London: Advanced Institute of Management Research.

Samuels, B. (2010), 'How American research universities spend their money', *Huffington Post*, 19 April.

Sanderson, M. (1972), *The Universities and British Industry1850–1970*, London: Routledge and Kegan Paul.

Shanmugalingam, S., Puttick, R. and Westlake, S. (2010), *Rebalancing Act*, London: National Endowment for Science, Technology and the Arts, June.

Shepherd, J. (2010), 'Universities could save £3 billion by outsourcing says thinktank', *Guardian*, 23 December: 11.

Shonfield, Andrew (1965), *Modern Capitalism*, Oxford: Oxford University Press.

Smith, S. (2010a), 'Our universities are standing on the brink of catastrophe', *Observer*, 13 June.

Smith S. (2010b), 'Keynote speech', Universities UK Members' Annual Conference, Cranfield University, 9 September.

Smith, S. (2010c), 'Where is the government's mandate to change the world of higher education?', *Guardian,* 19 October.

Smith, S. (2011), 'University funding is actually going up', *Guardian*, 22 March.

Stewart, K. (2009), 'Labour's record on inequality and the new opportunities White Paper', *Political Quarterly*, 80 (3): 427–33.

Sutton Trust (2004) *The Missing 3000: State school students under-represented at leading universities*, London: Sutton Trust, August.

Sutton Trust (2008), *Report to the National Council for Education Excellence: Increasing Higher Education Participation amongst Disadvantaged Young People and School in Poor Communities*, London: Sutton Trust, October.

Sutton Trust (2008a), *Knowing Where to Study? Fees, Bursaries and Fair Access*, London: Sutton Trust.

Sutton Trust (2008b), *University Admissions by Individual School*, London: Sutton Trust.

Sutton Trust (2009), *The Educational Backgrounds of Leading Lawyers, Journalists, Vice Chancellors, Politicians, Medics and Chief Executives: Submission to the Milburn Commission on Access to the Professions, March*

2009, London: Sutton Trust

Sutton Trust (2010a), *Responding to the New Landscape for University Access*, London: Sutton Trust.

Sutton Trust (2010b), *The Educational Backgrounds of Government Ministers in 2010*, London: Sutton Trust.

Tarbert, H., Tee, K. and Watson, R. (2008), 'The legitimacy of pay and performance comparisons: an analysis of UK university vice chancellors pay awards', *British Journal of Industrial Relations*, 46 (4): 771.

Tawney, R.H. (1943), 'The problem of the public schools', *Political Quarterly*, 4: 117–49.

Tawney, R.H. (1964a), *The Radical Tradition*, London: Penguin.

Tawney, R.H. (1964b), *Equality*, London: Unwin.

Taylor-Gooby, P. (2011), 'The UK welfare state going west', in N. Yeates, T.

Thompson, J. and Bekhradnia, B. (2010), 'The government's proposals for higher education funding and student finance – an analysis', Oxford: Higher Education Policy Institute Report. Available at: http://www. hepi.ac.uk/466-1875/The-government's-proposals-for-higher-education-fundingand-student-finance-%e2%80%93-an-analysis.html [accessed 26 July 2011].

Tilly, C. (1998), *Durable Inequality*, Berkeley, CA: University of California Press.

Trow, M. (2006), 'Reflections on the transition from elite to mass to universal access: forms and phases of higher education in modern societies since World War II', *International Handbook of Higher Education*, 18 (I); 243–80.

Turner, S. P. (2003), *Liberal Democracy 3.0: Civil Society in an Age of Experts*, London: Sage.

UK Commission for Employment and Skills (2010), *Skills for Jobs: Today and Tomorrow*, London: UK Commission for Employment and Skills, March.

UK Trade and Investment (2010), *UK Inward Investment 2009/10: The UK. At the Heart of Global Business*, London: UK Trade and Investment, July.

Universities UK (2010) *Making the Case for Higher Education in the Creative Economy*, London: Universities UK, December.

University and College Union (2009), 'Stand up for Research' petition to remove impact assessment from the Research Excellence Framework, *University and College Union*, http://www.ucu.org.uk/index. cfm?articleid=4207 [accessed 21 August 2011].

Vasagar, J. (2010a), 'Percentage of poor pupils admitted to Oxbridge – 1%', *Guardian*, 22 December.

Vasagar, J. (2010b). '21 Oxbridge colleges did not take black students', *Guardian*, 7 December.

Vogt, T., Baird, D. and Robinson, C. (2007), 'Opportunities in the postacademic world', *Nature Nanotechnology*, 2: 329–32.

Waldegrave, W. (1993) *Realising Our Potential: A Strategy for Science, Engineering and Technology*, London: HMSO, http://www.

officialdocuments.gov.uk/document/cm22/2250/2250.pdf [accessed 21 August2011].

Wallas, G. (1936), *The Great Society: A Psychological Analysis*, London: Macmillan.

Warry Report (2006), *Increasing the Economic Impact of Research Councils*, London: Research Council Economic Impact Group, http://www.bis.gov.uk/files/file32802.pdf [accessed 21 August 2011].

Washburn, J. (2005), *University Inc.: The Corporate Corruption of Higher Education*, New York, NY: Basic Books.

Weber, M. (1948 [1919]), 'Science as a vocation', in Max Weber, *From Max Weber: Essays in Sociology*, trans. and ed. H.H. Gerth and C. Wright Mills, London: Routledge and Kegan Paul.

White Paper (2011), *Securing a Sustainable Future for Higher Education: An Independent Review of Higher Education Funding and Student Finance*, London: HMSO. Available at: http://webarchive.nationalarchives.gov.uk/+/hereview.independent.gov.uk/hereview/ [accessed 25 July 2011].

Wilby, P. (2010), 'Ed Miliband is wrong. Tuition fees gave poorer students hope', *Guardian*, 7 December. Available at: http://www.guardian.co.uk/commentisfree/2010/dec/07/ed-miliband-tuition-fees-university [accessed 30 August 2011].

Wilkinson, R. and Pickett, K. (2009), *The Spirit Level: Why More Equal Societies Almost Always Do Better*, London: Allen Lane.

Willetts, D. (2010), *The Pinch: How the Baby Boomers Took their Children's Future – And Why They Should Give It Back*, London: Atlantic.

Wilson, F. R. (2006), *The Segregated Scholars: Black Social Scientists and the Creation of Black Labor Studies, 1890–1950*, Charlottesville, VA: University of Virginia Press.

Wolf, A. (2011), *Review of Vocational Education – The Wolf Report*, London: Department for Education. Available at: https://www.education.gov.uk/publications/eOrderingDownload/The%20Wolf%20Report.pdf [accessed 27 July 2011].

Ziman, J. (2000), *Real Science. What It Is, and What It Means*, Cambridge: Cambridge University Press.

Ziman, J. (2002), 'The continuing need for disinterested research', *Science and Engineering Ethics*, 8: 397–9.

Index